Helping My Hero!!

A Guide for Young Readers Whose Parents May Have Combat Trauma

**Written by Sherry Barron
and illustrated by Nick Adducci**

Helping My Hero!! © 2015 Campus Crusade for Christ, Inc. All rights reserved.

Helping My Hero!! A Guide for Young Readers Whose Parents May Have Combat Trauma, by Sherry Barron, is published by Cru Military. It is part of the **Bridges to Healing Series**. The material and book structure of *Helping My Hero!!* were adapted with permission from *When War Comes Home: Christ-centered Healing for Wives of Combat Veterans*, written by Chris and Rahnella Adsit and Marshéle Carter Waddell (© 2008, Campus Crusade for Christ, Inc.).

Limitations: No portion of this book may be reproduced, stored in a retrieval system or transmitted in any form or by any means – electronic, mechanical, photocopy, recording or any other – except for brief quotations in printed reviews or for educational purposes, without the prior written permission of the publisher.

Published by Cru Military, a division of Campus Crusade for Christ, Inc., 100 Lake Hart Drive, Orlando, FL 32832, USA. For more information about Cru Military, please visit our web site at www.crumilitary.org or call toll-free in the USA, 1-800-444-6006.

All Scripture quotations, unless noted otherwise, are taken from the Common English Bible, © 2010, 2011 by Common English Bible. Used by permission. All rights reserved worldwide.

Illustrations by Nick Adducci, BangarangAnimation.com

ISBN: 978-0-9863630-1-6
Printed in the United States of America

DISCLAIMER
This book is not a substitute for appropriate medical or psychological care for those experiencing significant emotional pain or whose ability to function at home, school or work is impaired. Chronic or extreme stress may cause a wide assortment of physical and psychological problems. Some may require evaluation and treatment by medical or mental health professionals. When in doubt, seek advice from a professional.

Table of Contents

Foreword	3
Letter to Readers	5
1 What Happened to Her Dad?	7
2 What Happened to Our Emotions?	15
3 Why is Everyone so Sad?	23
4 Is Dad Getting Better?	31
5 What Should We Do Next?	41
6 Is Anyone Listening?	49

7 How Can God Help?	61
8 How Can Friends Help?	71
9 Am I God's Child?	81
10 Who is My Enemy?	89
11 How Can I Help My Mom and Dad?	97
12 How Can We Help Others Our Age?	107
13 How Will It End?	117
Appendix	127

Foreword

Chances are you're holding this book and reading this forward because someone you love very much went to war and came home a different person. You also are feeling the effects of combat trauma.

Cru Military's **Bridges to Healing** project first focused on providing Christ-centered solutions for warriors coming home with spiritual wounds of combat trauma and Post-Traumatic Stress Disorder (PTSD). Author Chris Adsit wrote *The Combat Trauma Healing Manual* providing Biblical answers to address these wounds. Soon, realizing combat trauma affects the whole family and that wives face unique challenges, Chris Adsit, Rahnella Adsit and Marshéle Carter Waddell wrote *When War Comes Home*, providing factual information about combat trauma and PTSD. Its 13 chapters lead wives on a journey of healing for secondary trauma stress.

"Please get me something to help the children. They're getting lost." This was the cry of military chaplains from all branches when Cru Military asked, "How can we help you?"

With a passion to help military children, Sherry Barron used her experience as a military wife, mother, educator and author to write this book, *Helping My Hero!! A Guide for Young Readers Whose Parents May Have Combat Trauma*, for children in 4th-6th grades.

Following the 13-chapter format of *When War Comes Home*, this series of children's books also includes, *My Hero's Home!! A Guide for Young Children Whose Parents May Have Combat Trauma* (K-3rd grades), and *My Hero Hurts!! A Study Guide for Teenagers Whose Parents May Have Combat Trauma* (7th-12th grades). The Christ-centered solutions and unique formats in these books will help communication between parents and their children.

In addressing the effects of combat trauma on children, this book fulfills a vision we've had since the Vietnam War. We saw these effects firsthand while in the Army, as Cub Scout leaders and while teaching in the Department of Defense School in Schweinfurt, Germany. As we studied the stresses on our military families serving during the Afghanistan and Iraq wars, the vision became clear. We are very appreciative of Cru Military, their financial supporters and Sherry Barron for making this vision a reality. We pray you receive spiritual healing from the Christ-centered solutions in this book.

Ron and Marcy Wheat
Cru Military Missionaries

Dear Young Readers,

We think you will enjoy reading the story of two military families and their experiences of dealing with Post-Traumatic Stress Disorder or Combat Trauma. Included in each chapter will be oodles of information to educate you on the realities many families are dealing with because of intense war situations.

You will meet Sara, a sixth-grader, her brother, Jacob, who is in fifth grade, and Jenna, Sara's best friend from school. Their fathers have just returned from long deployments. They love living in the same neighborhood and see each other every day. You will also meet Barney, a loving and devoted German shepherd, who has been with Sara and Jacob since he was a playful puppy.

You will find stories, activities, questions to answer and so much more. There are many things you can talk over with your mom or dad.

You will also find God-solutions to some very tough situations many families are going through because of war. We believe you will find excellent information to help you and your whole family.

Sherry Barron
Sherry Barron and the Cru Military Team
www.crumilitary.org

Chapter 1
Story by Jenna

Someone kept ringing the doorbell over and over again. It was almost annoying until I looked out the little peephole to see my best friend, Sara, crying and getting ready to pound on the door. "Sara!" I yelled as the door flew open. "What's the matter? Why are you crying?" Sara ran into the front hallway and could barely get any understandable words out. "My dad just got arrested by the military police ... He was waving a gun at my mom!"

"What?? That can't be! Sara, what happened? Tell me exactly," I said. Sobbing while she spoke to me, Sara blurted out her story. Just as she started, my mom came to see what all the noise was. She had been in the backyard doing some gardening. "Hello, Mrs. Poole." Sara could barely get the words out. Mom wrapped her arms around Sara's shoulders and we all walked into the living room and sat down.

"Jenna, please get some Kleenex for Sara."

Waiting until I returned with the tissues, Sara began her story. She bent down to pet our beagle, that came and sat right in front of her with a look of concern in his eyes. Our dog always loved it whenever Sara came over.

After wiping the tears from her face, Sara began to speak, "When the bus dropped me off at the corner, I saw Dad's truck in the driveway. He never comes home in the middle of the day. When I saw the truck, I ran all the way home. As I got closer to the house, I could hear my mom and dad. Oh, Jenna! They were yelling at each other. They were saying such bad things. I didn't know if I should go inside; so first I peeked in the front window and saw that my dad had a gun aimed at my mom!!"

"Sara! What did you do?" I asked.

"I screamed and they heard me and saw me standing outside looking in. Dad ran upstairs as soon as he saw me."

Sara was speaking so fast, she had to pause to catch her breath.

"Mom grabbed her cell phone and ran outside to be with me. I was shaking so hard I could barely walk. Mom grabbed my hand, and we ran around the corner to Mom's friend's house. Lucky for us, she was home. Mom called the military police and they came right away."

"When they arrived, Mom told the MP's what had happened, and they ran out the front door grabbing for their guns," Sara exclaimed.

"Mom told me to ride her friend's bike over here to be with you. Is that OK?" asked Sara.

As I glanced at Mom, she said, "Sara, your mom just called and told me you were on your way. Of course, you can stay with us as long as is needed. I see you have your backpack. Do you girls have homework to do?"

"Yes, we always have homework, Mom!" I said with a big sigh.

"Let's go in the kitchen while I make you a snack," said Mom. By now, Sara had stopped crying, but the sad look on her face was hard to miss.

"Mom, what happened to Sara's dad? Why is he acting this way?" I asked as we hopped up on the stools. Just then the phone rang and Mom answered it. She walked into the living room talking softly to someone. When she came back into the kitchen, she told us Sara's dad had been arrested peacefully and taken away by the military policemen.

Sara's mom had to go do some paperwork so Mom said Sara could spend the night at our house.

When I heard that, I was wondering if it had anything to do with what Sara's dad was doing when he was overseas. He had just come back from the war about a month ago. Sara told me he had been acting so strangely. He did not look at her like he used to or want to do anything fun.

I wonder what all those differences are? Is _my_ dad going to be different when he comes home in a few months?

What is ...

causing the abnormal or unusual behavior?

(aiming a gun at a loved one)

Answer: Many men and women serving in the war zone come back home with stress due to Combat Trauma. With proper training, many people have found ways to deal with the wounds of war but some stress injuries take a long time to heal. If not properly understood, the symptoms and abnormal behavior can last over many weeks. Sometimes they can cause troubling events to happen for the family.

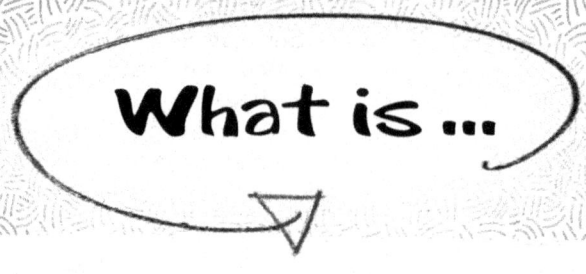

this strange behavior called?
(Post-Traumatic Stress [PTS] or Combat Trauma)

Answer: Post-Traumatic Stress (PTS) can show up whenever any kind of horrible event makes a person think they will be injured or killed. Besides combat, experiences such as abuse, accidents, news of a terrible illness, severe weather conditions or seeing a person die can cause symptoms of PTS to occur. If the symptoms last a long time, the person may be diagnosed with PTSD (Post-Traumatic Stress Disorder). Even those who go to the war zone but are not fighting the enemy up front can be affected by what they see, smell, hear and feel through the harsh experiences of war.

God's Words

When I Am Afraid

"The Lord is my strength and my shield. My heart trusts Him. I was helped, my heart rejoiced, and I thank Him with my song."

~ Psalm 28:7

"God is our refuge and strength, a help always near in times of great trouble. That's why we won't be afraid when the world falls apart."

~ Psalm 46:1,2a

Discoveries

Signs to Help You See ...
what symptoms your wounded parent may have.

(Check the ones you have observed)

- ____ Nightmares
- ____ Always talking about the war zone
- ____ Eyes that don't see me even when looking at me
- ____ Does not want to do any fun activities
- ____ Gets angry easily when driving
- ____ Always seems to be sad
- ____ Comes home from work and goes straight to bed
- ____ Plays music too loud
- ____ Reacts easily to loud noises
- ____ Drinks beer/alcohol too much
- ____ Does not sleep all night
- ____ Seems to be mad for no reason

POSITIVE ACTIVITIES

- Find out more about PTSD so I can understand and help Sara.
- Be an encourager to Sara, her mom and brother.
- Pray for Sara's dad to get better and get the help he needs.
- Invite Sara's family to church.
- Ask Mom if she would make a meal to take over to the family.
- Try to sit by Sara on the bus and at the lunch table every day.
- Be a good listener.
- Design a "Hope You're Doing Better" card for Sara's family.
- Make Sara a special bracelet she can wear to remind her to pray for her dad.
- Pick a bouquet of flowers and give to Sara's mom.

Jenna's Prayer

"Dear Lord, wow! I'm not sure how to pray for Sara and her family, but I know You will help them with their big problem. They say Sara's dad has some PTSD symptoms so I pray the right people will be available to give him all the right kind of care he needs to get 100% better. Help me know how to be available whenever I can do something that shows I care. Please heal Sara's dad so he can come back home real soon. Amen"

 ## The Important Life Value is:

Commitment
    (definition: to make a pledge or a promise)

I promise to be there while Sara's family goes through this big test.
I commit to pray for Sara and especially her father, every night before falling asleep.

signed, Jenna

What Happened to Our Emotions?

Chapter 2
Story by Sara

These have been the longest two months in my life! It seems like just yesterday that Jenna and her mom helped me when I saw Dad with the gun. I don't understand why I feel so sad and mad at the same time. Dad has to live in a different place, and I haven't seen him since the police came. I don't even know who I am mad at but my tummy always feels upset at something.

"Hello," I said, as I picked up our ringing phone.

Mom was running errands and I had just gotten home from school.

"Sara, it's Jenna. Have you thought of what to write for our English assignment with Mr. Reed?"

"No, I just got home. Give me a break! I haven't even had a chance to get my books out of my backpack." Jenna was excited about something so I let her talk.

"I was talking to Mom about our assignment and she had the best idea. She thought it would be great if you and I write about what we find out about Post-Traumatic Stress Disorder. We could each take a different angle on the topic. What do you think?"

Ever since Mom told me that Dad had some testing done and the doctors had put a name to it, I was curious about what that meant exactly. "Jenna, that's a great idea. Wait 'til I get paper and a pen. I have to write those words down so I won't forget which word comes first. Hang on."

"Oh, where is some paper and a pen when I need it," I mumbled out loud searching through the drawer by the phone. "Okay. I found something to write on. What is that called again?"

Jenna said slowly, "Post ... Traumatic ... Stress ... Disorder. Did you get it all?"

"Yes, thanks. When my mom comes back, I'll ride my bike over and we can get started doing some research. Okay? I have to ask permission first."

Just then, I heard the garage door open.

"Jenna, I'll call you right back. My mom just got home."

I know Mom will like the idea of writing about what Dad is suffering from. When I went into the garage through the kitchen door, Mom was just opening the driver's door of her car.

"Mom, can I ride my bike over to Jenna's right now? We are going to work on a writing project we have for school. Jenna's mom had this great idea to write about ..." I had to look at the note in my hand. "Post-Traumatic Stress Disorder. We have to do some research. Is it okay with you?"

Mom had such a startled look on her face as she set the grocery bags down on the counter. She pulled some books out of one of the bags. "Sara, you won't believe it! I just brought home some books on PTSD. You can use them for your research. Yes, you can go but be back by 6 o'clock. Call me before you leave Jenna's, so I know when you are on your way home."

This is amazing. The books are really going to help us learn some important facts. Maybe the information will help me understand why I feel the way I feel all the time. As I put the books in my backpack, I saw Mom standing by the sink looking out the kitchen window. "Mom, will Dad ever get to come home again?"

As she turned to look at me, there were tears in her eyes. "I hope so, Sara," she said. "I hope so."

What is...

happening to Sara's emotions right now?
(feeling sad and mad and not knowing why)

Answer: Family members can experience Secondary Traumatic Stress after witnessing or hearing about something terrible that has happened. Some of the symptoms are listed below. Check the boxes of the ones you have felt recently. From the list, pick out the top three that bother you the most.

- ❏ Confused
- ❏ Bad Dreams
- ❏ Fearful
- ❏ Moody
- ❏ Upset Tummy

- ❏ Forgetful
- ❏ Angry
- ❏ Sad
- ❏ Sleepless
- ❏ Lonely

1. _____
2. _____
3. _____

What is... the best way for Sara to feel better about her situation?

(feeling hopeless and afraid she will never be happy again)

Answer:

- Find a 'Battle Buddy' (a caring friend) who understands and cares about what is happening in her family.

- Make Christ an important part of the healing from stress. (See Chapter Six to learn how.)

- Take time to rest and have some fun with her family or a friend.

- Take time to read a chapter a day from the book of Psalms in the Bible.

- Take all her troubles to the Lord in prayer, every day.

- Set her schedule for the day and stick to it.

- Practice being patient with the realities of life.

- Seek to do something nice for someone without being asked.

- Learn to forgive even when it looks hopeless.

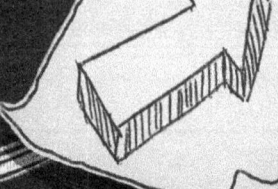

God's Words

When I Am Sad

"Why, I ask myself, are you so depressed? Why are you so upset inside? Hope in God! Because I will again give Him thanks, my saving presence and my God."

~ Psalm 42:5

"Cast your burden on the Lord – He will support you! God will never let the righteous be shaken!"

~ Psalm 55:22

Discoveries

What Sara and Jenna learned from their writing assignment:

Post-Traumatic Stress Disorder

- **PTSD** is the most severe form of Combat Trauma.
- **PTSD** is a common reaction to an uncommon event. It is common for those who saw, smelled, felt, heard and tasted things of war to be acting very differently from how they normally would..
  - It is not unusual for someone to be affected by the combat of war and by threat, trauma, pain, atrocity, horror, gore and loss.
  - Facing death changes a person.
- **PTSD** is not a sign of weakness. Instead it reveals the signs of a wound.
  - The word "trauma" is from a Greek word which means "a wounding."
  - A psychological wound can change emotions, cause people to lose faith, lose self-identity, lose confidence, lose trust in others, and lose their sense of security.
- **PTSD** has been called many names over the centuries: The Swiss called it "nostalgia." The Germans called it "Heimweh" (homesickness), The French called it "maladie du pays" (homesickness), and the Spanish called it "estar roto" (to be broken). During the American Civil War it was called "soldier's heart." During World War I it was called "shell-shocked." During World War II it was called "combat fatigue." During the Korean War it was called "war neurosis," and in the 1970's psychiatrists called it "Vietnam Veterans Syndrome." In 1980 the term officially became "**Post-Traumatic Stress Disorder**."
- The shock of war experiences causes a reaction in a person's hormonal balance.
  - An **adrenaline rush** causes the heart to beat faster, lungs to pump harder, and the pupils in the eyes to dilate or grow larger.
  - 70% of the **oxygen** normally sent to the **brain** now shoots out to the muscles so they can be ready to run or get away from danger.
  - The brain works overtime to record the bad memories so they can be avoided in the future.
  - The lower brain now takes over and gets the mind, body and soul ready for whatever it takes to **survive**.

POSITIVE ACTIVITIES

- Challenge Mom to read the books on PTSD with me so we can talk about what we learn.
- Ask Mr. Reed if Jenna and I can read our reports to the class.
- Make a batch of cookies and find out how to get them to Dad.
- Write a letter to Dad every Saturday to let him know what happened each week at home.
- Make sure my brother Jacob understands what is happening to all of us because of Dad's condition.
- Take some photos of each of us doing different activities to send to Dad.
- Encourage Dad to write a journal of what he is learning through this experience.
- Tell Dad we are praying that God will heal him from PTSD.
- Pray for Dad every day.
- Ask Mom if we can go visit Dad.

Sara's Prayer

"Dear God, I am asking You to come and help my family, especially my dad. We are all sad because he came back from overseas so different. Please help him get better so he can come and live with us again. Please help him see he needs You, God. Heal him from his wounds inside his mind and heart. Amen."

 The Important Life Value is:

Loyalty
  (definition: to be completely devoted
  and faithful)

I want to be devoted to my dad and his healing.
I want to faithfully pray for our family to be better after all of this is over.
I don't want to give up on Dad, but I want to be loyal to him no matter what happens.

  signed, Sara

Chapter 3
Story by Jacob

I wasn't even home when the police came to take my dad to jail.

I wonder what really happened to make him act that way with the gun. Mom and Sara seem to be keeping secrets from me because whenever I ask them a question, they always have this look between them. That look always makes me feel so confused. "Mom, can you and Sara not have that look you always have when I ask about Dad? I just want to know what's happening, that's all. It seems like our family is falling apart." Mom came over to the stool where I sat doing homework and gave me a big hug.

"Jacob, we're not doing anything on purpose. It must be frustrating for you not to know all the details. I guess I have wanted to keep some of the information from you so you won't be afraid. Your father has to stay away for a while. There were many things which happened this time when he went overseas that hurt his heart and mind."

"But Mom, he didn't get shot or blown up in a jeep, did he?" I asked. Barney looked at me with concern.

"No, but there are wounds that hurt just as much because of the things that happen in a war situation. Dad was in a place where there was a lot of fighting with the enemy." Mom sat down on the stool next to me. She grabbed a book from the kitchen table and opened it up. She read silently for a minute before speaking again.

"Your dad came home this time with a condition called Post-Traumatic Stress Disorder. When he had the gun aimed at me, he thought he was back in the war. His mind was playing tricks on him. The doctors are helping him with counseling and medicines, and are keeping him busy with appointments. He has to make some improvements before we can go visit him."

"Mom, I don't understand why it is taking so long. I wish my heart would stop hurting so much."

"Let me explain why your father is not here at home and is staying at the Wounded Warrior dormitory for now. It is like when he goes through special training to prepare for war. But, now he is being trained in how to best manage his feelings. Does that make sense?"

"Why can't he live at home?" I asked. Barney came and put his paw on my leg because of my shaky voice.

"The gun and the arrest happened before the doctors knew his condition and that's what's keeping him from coming home yet. He has to show he is capable of controlling his emotions. Even though he won't be able to have a gun in the house, he must show improvement first," said Mom. She told me to look her in the eyes. She said she wanted to make me a promise.

"Jacob, whenever you have a question, I promise to answer it to the best of my ability. You, Sara and I can sit down and discuss some of the information we have learned about Dad's condition. I'm still learning how to deal with it myself. What do you say?" Barney came close to us, wagging his tail.

"OK, Mom, but please don't have that look you guys have 'cause it makes me feel weird. I feel lonely or something 'cause you and Sara know more than I do. It makes me feel like I'm still a baby!"

 # What is ...

the reason Jacob feels so alone?

(feeling like nobody cares that he wants to know what is happening with his dad)

Answer: Each member of the family is dealing with their dad's condition in a different way. Because of the loss of the way their relationship used to be, Jacob's family is experiencing grief. The word "grief" comes from the Latin verb meaning "to burden." Grief can feel like a huge load that is too heavy to carry. Jacob's mom is now without her husband and has to wait to see if he will heal from his wounds.

Sara is dealing with her loss by studying as much as she can about the topic of PTSD. Jacob needs to feel like he is included in all of the steps leading to improvement in his dad's life. The loss itself is not the problem, but the process of getting from realizing there is an issue to waiting for a good result is difficult.

What is ...

the "Grief Cycle"?

(the cycle of emotional ups and downs any person goes through when there is significant loss)

Answer: 7 Stages of Grief

Each person goes through the following stages of grief differently no matter what their age. It is normal for anyone to be depressed and sad. Others may not understand, and want you to get "over it." A later stage could involve a period of wanting to be isolated and alone so you can deal with everything. Here is the grief model:

1. Shock and Denial

A person may react to learning of a loss with numbed disbelief. Denial that anything has happened is normal in order to avoid the pain of the loss. Shock provides protection from being overwhelmed with emotions all at once. It could be weeks before it wears off.

2. Pain and Guilt

The pain sets in as the shock wears off. Realize the pain should be felt as part of the grieving process. A person may think it is something they said or did that caused the loss. This phase may have unexpectedly chaotic or scary times.

3. Anger and Bargaining

Frustration at the situation gives way to angry outbursts. Close relationships may be harmed if the anger is not controlled. There could be bargaining episodes which go something like this, "I will always keep my room clean and then Dad can come home."

4. Depression, Reflection, Loneliness

People close to someone grieving may wonder why it is taking so long for them to heal from their loss. A long period of sad reflection may take over those who are grieving. Usually when the reality of the situation sets in, they tend to isolate themselves on purpose. They want to think about the things they did with their loved one.

5. The Upward Turn

As the new way of life takes place, life can become calmer and more organized. The physical symptoms mentioned in the previous stages may lessen and the depression can begin to fade away.

6. Rebuild and Work Through

Open communication is key to the family moving forward in a positive way. Getting into a regular routine will keep those painful emotions from taking over. Working on projects and problem solving will keep everyone in the family on the right track to complete healing.

7. Acceptance and Hope

Life has changed and there will come a time when acceptance of the situation takes place. Acceptance does not necessarily mean complete happiness and no more sadness. When everyone in the family has come to this stage, hope of a brighter future should happen.

God's Words

When I Feel Alone

"The Lord is close to everyone who calls out to Him, to all who call out to Him sincerely."

~ Psalm 145:18

"Even when I walk through the darkest valley, I fear no danger because You are with me. Your rod and Your staff – they protect me."

~ Psalm 23:4

Discoveries
Am I Grieving or Not??

Symptoms of grieving for any kind of loss can look like the following:

(Circle any that apply to you)

Fear

Crying

Feeling abandoned

No desire to talk

Rage

Anger

Sleepiness

Loss of appetite

Frustrated

Nightmares

Loss of faith

Blaming others

Talking too much

Running away

Loneliness

Feeling out of control

No feelings at all

Guilt

POSITIVE ACTIVITIES

- When asked, "How are you?" give a positive answer such as "I'm getting better day by day!"
- Obey my mom the first time she asks me to do something.
- Pray for my dad every day, especially that he will continue to work on getting better.
- Make a paper airplane out of a letter I've written to Dad and mail it in a big enough envelope to not bend it.
- Tell Mom that when I feel so sad, it hurts too much.
- Write my feelings daily in the journal Mom gave me.
- Reach out to other boys I know whose fathers have PTSD.
- Read my Bible every day.
- Write a "Dreams I Have" list of what I want to see change in the future for our family.
- Read a book about PTSD in order to understand what's happened to Dad.

Jacob's Prayer

"Dear God, thank You for understanding my pain and loneliness. I pray for You to help me get through this loss of our normal family life. I pray You will give us the hope we need for a better future. Heal my dad. Give Mom and Sara and me peace like only You can give. Amen."

⊕ The Important Life Value is:

Contentment
(definition: to have peace of mind and to be satisfied with the situation)

I want to be content with our new family life. I want to be content in the hope we will have my dad home again soon. I want to be thankful God will heal my dad and his heart wound.

signed, Jacob

30

Chapter 4
Story by Sara

Dad has been living away from home for over four months now. My birthday is coming soon and when Mom gets home from work I'm going to ask her if he can come to the party. I wonder what he will be like? Will he even want to come home and have fun with us again?

Just then, I heard the garage door open, so I ran to throw open the door leading to the garage. Before Mom could get out of the car I ran to the driver's door. "Mom? Mom, can we invite Dad to my birthday party?" I rattled off so fast, that Mom had a surprised look on her face.

"Say again, Sara, I did not understand a word you said. You spoke too-oo-oo fast!" laughed Mom as she climbed out of the car, grabbing her purse and a notebook from the passenger seat.

"I said, 'Could we invite Dad to come home for my birthday party in two weeks?'" This time I slowed down, and said each word more deliberately.

"Let me get in the house and change clothes, and we'll sit down and discuss your idea. Okay?" Mom said.

"Okay. Should I call Jacob in from the backyard, too? Remember, he wants to know what's going on when it involves something with Dad."

As she walked down the hallway to her bedroom, Mom said, "I'll just be a minute or two. Why don't you guys get some cookies and milk and bring them out to the patio table."

My mind was racing with ideas and I ran to my room to get a pad of paper and a pencil. It would be so neat if we wrote Dad a letter and, if Mom likes the invitation idea, we could all sign the letter. Mom had made fresh chocolate chip cookies last night, so I filled a plate with them, grabbed glasses and the milk carton, and put everything on a tray. Jacob and I sat at the outdoor table enjoying our snack while we waited for Mom to come outside.

When she came out to the patio, Mom had the notebook in her hand that she'd brought in from the car. She didn't say anything until she opened up to a certain page. I was really curious what she it had written down that was so important for our little talk.

Mom poured herself some milk, grabbed a cookie and dunked it into the glass. "Mmm, love these cookies! Okay, before we start talking about Dad coming to the birthday party, I have some news about him. I was meeting with Chaplain Johnson this morning and these are the notes I took."

"Mom, does it mean Dad gets to come home for good?"

"Not exactly, but Dad has shown lots of improvement and has been getting help in dealing with the wounds he has from his last deployment. Jacob, even though you cannot see the wounds, they are hidden deep in his mind and heart. Those kinds of wounds have to heal just as if he had a broken leg. Remember when you broke your wrist skateboarding and you had to wear the cast for six weeks? Dad also needs time for his pain to heal."

"What did the chaplain tell you about Dad, Mom? I asked.

"Well, he told me Dad could come home for a visit, so when we have the party that would be a perfect time. We'll go to the dormitory where he has been staying and pick him up for the day.

"The military police have already taken all the hunting guns out of our home. That is one of the rules for his visit. And he has some homework from his therapy, that he needs to do with us. The party will be a good positive activity but we can't have any balloons in case they pop and make a loud noise. A bang like that can be a trigger, and we don't want to cause Dad to have any stress. What do you say? Does that sound like a good idea?"

Sara thought for a minute and said, "Mom, we can make these two parties in one! We can have a celebration party for Dad coming home for a visit and a birthday party for me!"

Mom smiled real big and jumped up to give me a big hug. Then she went to Jacob's chair and grabbed him for a hug too. And then she grabbed both of us together and we had a three-way hug. Barney wanted some love too so we all bent down to pet and hug our eager German shepherd. As Mom sat down again, she said there was one more thing she wanted to tell us about her talk with the chaplain.

"Dad has been working hard on some assignments, almost like doing homework. He has been waiting until just the right time to come home because he wants to speak to all of us about forgiveness. Chaplain Johnson has been helping him with some studies found in the Bible. The topic this week has been forgiveness, and it is important for your dad to ask for your forgiveness because of the scare he gave us. We are going to let him come earlier than your birthday guests so we can have some alone time together as a family. What do you think?"

"Oh, Mom, that sounds so good. I really miss being with Dad. We used to have so much fun together," I said.

Jacob jumped up from his chair, ran out into the yard to grab his baseball glove and yelled as he ran back, "We can play catch, too!"

What is...

forgiveness?

(to recognize there should be a face-to-face confrontation to say "I'm sorry" for an offense)

Answer:

- It says "I'm sorry" for something bad that has been done.
- It makes amends for a wrong.
- It is the first step to healing.
- It benefits everyone.
- It releases unhealthy anger.
- It frees the forgiver.
- It helps the forgiver and the forgiven one make things right.
- It is a learned behavior.
- It leads to asking for forgiveness if needed.

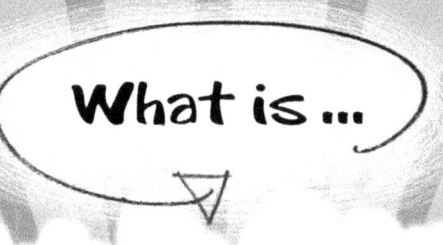

written about forgiveness in the Bible?

(It is important to know how to ask for forgiveness and to know how to forgive.)

Answer:

- Ask for forgiveness. It is important to say the right words such as "I am sorry. I was wrong. Will you forgive me for getting angry with you this morning?" (or for whatever the offense was).
- To forgive someone, you could say, "I forgive you for your anger." (It is important to forgive even if you don't feel like it.)
- What to say if you both need to ask forgiveness: "I forgive you. I am sorry. I was wrong for saying those bad words toward you too. Will you forgive me?" (This is very helpful in giving the relationship a fresh start.)
- Always work on relationships so bitterness does not have a hold on you and others.

God's Words

When I Need to Forgive

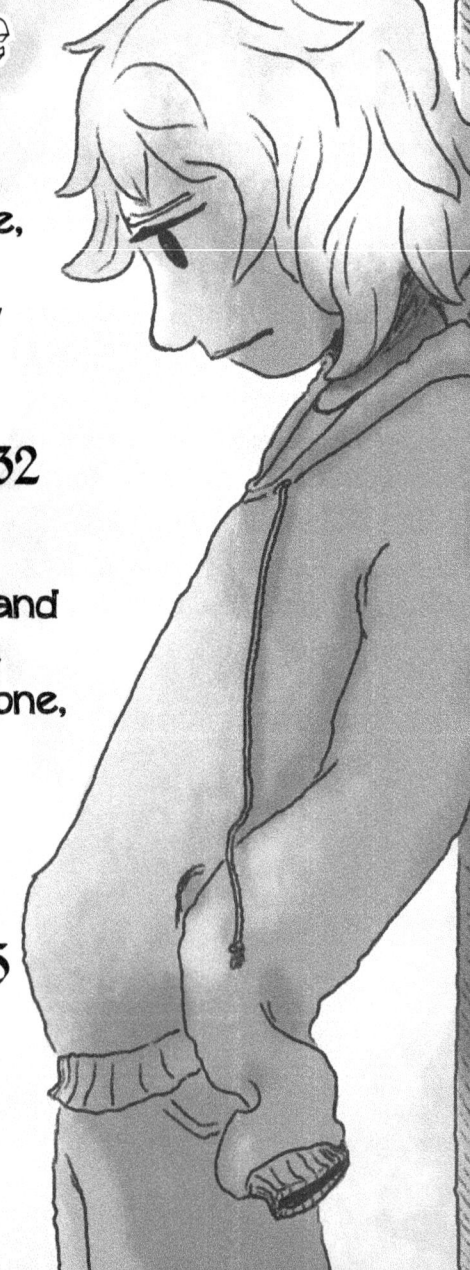

"Be kind, compassionate, and forgiving to each other, in the same way God forgave you in Christ."
~ Ephesians 4:32

"And whenever you stand up to pray, if you have something against anyone, forgive so that your Father in heaven may forgive you your wrongdoings."
~ Mark 11:25

Discoveries

Types of Wrongs I Should Say I'm Sorry for:

Note: Look up the verses and write out in
your own words what each verse means to you.

1. Being angry at others. .... Matthew 5:22
   _____
   _____

2. Being bitter when I don't get my way all the time .... Ephesians 4:31
   _____
   _____

3. Loving anything more than God. .... Exodus 20:3
   _____
   _____

4. Not respecting my mother and father .... Exodus 20:12
   _____
   _____

5. Stealing something belonging to another .... Exodus 20:15
   _____
   _____

6. Lying to my parents, teachers and others .... Exodus 20:16
   _____
   _____

7. Being greedy of my possessions .... Ephesians 4:19
   _____
   _____

8. Not being kind to my friends and neighbors .... Romans 13:10
   _____
   _____

9. Being more proud of what I can do than what others can do .... James 4:16,17
   _____
   _____

10. Being selfish as opposed to being caring and helpful ...... 2 Timothy 3:2
    _____
    _____

POSITIVE ACTIVITIES

- Make our home a welcoming place for Dad.
- Make Dad's favorite meal and dessert for our time together.
- Be ready to forgive Dad when he comes home for the first time.
- Pray for Dad to have complete healing.
- Ask Dad if he wants to go to church together as a family.
- Get a nice gift for Dad that we can give him to welcome him home.
- Besides decorating for the birthday party, make a "welcome home" sign, too.
- Just hug and love on Dad as much as possible.
- Clean our rooms so they look very neat for Dad.
- Ask nicely to see if Dad wants to play catch or some other kind of game.

Sara's Prayer

"Dear God, thank You that our dad will be coming home soon for a visit. Please heal him from what has given him so much pain that he can't live with us right now. Help us to be the kind of family which forgives and asks for forgiveness when we need to. We are counting on You to help us be a family again. We love You. Amen."

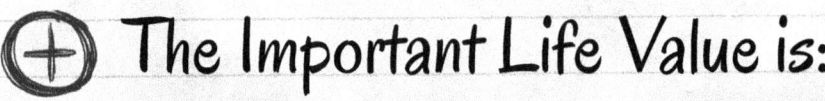 **The Important Life Value is:**

Responsibility
 (definition: to be reliable and dependable in a situation)

Our desire is we will all take responsibility for our part when asking for forgiveness and forgiving others when we've been wronged. We want to draw closer to God so He can help us be the kind of people who are kind, caring, compassionate and loving.

signed, Sara, Jacob and Mom

Chapter 5
Story by Jenna

Sara's birthday party was so much fun. At first, when I saw her dad at the party, I did not know what to think. My surprised look made my friend pull me into her bedroom to tell me what was happening.

Sara blurted out as she shut her door on the party, "Jenna, my dad came home and asked us all to forgive him for his bad behavior. He still has to live someplace else but Chaplain Johnson is giving him homework to do so he can get better! Isn't that cool?"

"Oh, Sara, I'm so happy for your family. Oh my gosh, I have so many questions in my mind. What made him act that way with the gun? Did he ever tell you?" I asked.

"First of all, I found out my mom has been meeting with Chaplain Johnson and she has this great notebook filled with ideas of how we as his family can help him. We've been having some family talk times to prepare us for today," Sara said.

Suddenly, we heard a knock, knock, knock at the door which startled both of us. Sara peeked around the door to see Jacob standing there. He yelled, "Mom said you should come back to the party and not be in your room 'cause more friends are here!"

"Jenna, let's ask Mom if you can spend the night, and we'll have more time to talk. Call your mom to see if you can, okay?" Sara said as she walked out the door.

When I called Mom, she said it was fine. I went home after the party to get my sleeping stuff. While I was there, the phone rang and I heard Mom answer it. I waited till she was done before saying good-bye.

"Who called?" I asked, while walking toward the front door to leave. "Jenna, you're not going to believe this, but it was a reporter from the Channel Seven news program. He got our name from the Family Readiness Officer of your dad's unit. They want to interview us because we are a family waiting for our loved one to return from being overseas for so long. They want to know how we are preparing ourselves to make the transition from being without Dad to having him home, when he comes back," Mom said with an astonished sound in her voice.

"You mean they're coming here with cameras and microphones and all that stuff? When?" I asked excitedly. Mom said they'd be here tomorrow around three o'clock. They're going to do the interview and photoshoot right in our living room. I can't wait to tell Sara and her mom.

"Bye, Mom, I'm going to the sleepover at Sara's," I said as I swung my backpack onto my back. When I pulled up on my bike in front of my friend's home, I saw Sara's mom and dad leaving in their car. She must be taking him back to wherever he's been living these past few months. I can't wait to find out what's been happening since the scary day with the gun. After grabbing a snack from the kitchen, Sara and I went straight to her room and closed the door. We put on some music on her laptop and sat down on the floor with our backs against the bed. Sara looked happy but I could still see some uncertainty in her eyes.

"So, Sara, what's been happening with your dad?" I asked. "Are you allowed to tell me?"

"When I asked Mom if you could come over, she gave me permission to tell you what we have learned, but she asked if you could just discuss it with your mom and no one else. Do you agree to do that?" she asked.
I said, "Of course, you can count on me to keep it private. Start at the beginning." I really wanted to know what caused the problems Sara's dad is having because my dad is coming home soon. It worries me that he might have some of the same behaviors as Sara's dad.

What is ...

the main reason Sara's dad had a gun aimed at his wife?

(the behavior is abnormal or not at all what is normal)

Answer: Sometimes the reactions military personnel have after coming back home from deployment are delayed for some time, even months. Sara's dad had an episode where he thought he was back in the battle. He and his family did not realize he had come home with an invisible wound of the heart and mind. He may have been praised for a job well done while serving overseas, but now he may be dealing with the reality of what happened during some of his fights with the enemy. If the spiritual side is not taken care of before going to war, during the battles of war and upon returning home, then some wounds of war will not heal. Sara's family must be educated on what is really happening and how to have the hope that leads to a happy life again.

What is...

the best way to prepare for the return of my father from being at war?

(having a family effort makes the transition as smooth as possible)

Answer: Write out the verse and jot down ideas of how to prepare for your family's situation.

1. **T**ake every situation to God in prayer .... Matthew 6:7,8
   _____
   _____
   _____

2. **R**ealize we must be patient .... Colossians 3:12
   _____
   _____
   _____

3. **U**nconditionally love, no matter what .... Ephesians 4:2
   _____
   _____
   _____

4. **S**ee how we can encourage others .... Romans 12:8
   _____
   _____
   _____

5. **T**rust God for every detail .... Proverbs 3:5,6
   _____
   _____
   _____

God's Words

When I Need Direction

"Every Scripture is inspired by God and is useful for teaching, for showing mistakes, for correcting, and for training character, so that the person who belongs to God can be equipped to do everything that is good."

~ 2 Timothy 3:16,17

"But anyone who needs wisdom should ask God, whose very nature is to give to everyone without a second thought, without keeping score. Wisdom will certainly be given to those who ask."

~ James 1:5

Discoveries
Know the Signs of Potential Triggers or Stressors

Note: If you see several of the following signs in your loved one's life, have a discussion with your healthy parent or guardian. Show them this list and let your parent deal with the situation. It is <u>not</u> your responsibility to take care of the problem, but you can be a part of the family team to help your parent who has PTSD symptoms heal from their wounds. The following list will help you be more informed and know there is hope for healing in the future.

TRIGGERS

- Anger
- Anxiety
- Sadness
- Feeling lonely
- Feeling abandoned
- Frustration
- Feeling vulnerable
- Feeling out of control
- Racing heartbeat
- Pain and muscle tension

STRESSORS

1. An action that causes the heart to pound
2. Anything that causes breathing problems
3. Anything that causes excess sweating
4. Showing signs of isolation
5. Loss of memory
6. Loss of interest in normal activities
7. Unable to show affection
8. Having unreasonable behavior
9. Being ever watchful
10. Being easily startled

POSITIVE ACTIVITIES

- Pray as a family for the safe return of my dad and healing of Sara's dad.
- Make a huge WELCOME HOME! sign to put on the garage door for my dad's return.
- Write a "Tribute to Dad" and have it framed to give to him when he comes home.
- Help Mom clean the house and make everything look great for Dad's return.
- Offer to work in the yard with Mom to pull weeds and mow the lawn.
- Write "I Love You because ..." notes and leave them in places where Dad will find them.
- Make a "Funny Jokes Our Family Loves" booklet to give to Dad.
- Make a special "Photo Album Just For Dad" using photos taken while he was away.
- Make a special dessert and take over to Sara's family.
- Give Mom extra hugs as we wait the last couple of weeks before Dad comes home.

Jenna's Prayer

"Dear God, thank You so much for keeping my dad safe. Help us be the kind of family that reaches out to others who have lost loved ones or have PTSD. Help us show love in little ways to those who are worried. Help our family share about how You want to give hope to others. We could not do this without You. Amen"

⊕ The Important Life Value is:

Endurance
(definition: the ability or strength to continue or last)

I want to be the kind of person who is available for my friends, my family and especially for God, whenever I am needed. I trust God will help me to endure.

signed, Jenna

Chapter 6
Story by Jacob

We had such a good time when Dad came home to help celebrate Sara's birthday. At first I felt really shy because I was afraid I would say something wrong. Dad was so happy to see us that he gave each one of us a five-minute bear hug. The smile on Mom's face was so big. It was great to see her very, very happy, because I have seen her crying quietly when she did not know I was looking.

Dad told us to sit down and listen, because he had something important he wanted to talk about with us. He started out by saying, "I've been learning a lot about myself and why I had the gun episode here at home. I know it scared you and I feel really bad it happened."

I leaned down to pet Barney, who had come to lie down next to my chair. I felt lucky to have such a great dog. He's been mine to take care of since I was five years old. Barney could tell something was not right.

Dad started talking again, "The time I had overseas this time was very difficult. I saw much more action as far as the combat fighting was concerned, and I had some close calls. Several of my buddies and men in my unit were either shot or blown up in their Humvees. I thought I was handling it alright over there and here, after returning, but I see now that was not the case."

"Dad, were you scared?" I asked.

"Sure, son, I was scared. But we get the best training and I was confident we could do a good job. What I didn't see coming was how it would affect me after I came back from this deployment," Dad admitted.

"I've been meeting with Chaplain Johnson every week since I went to live in the dorm. He has been helping me study the Bible and learn more about how God can help me heal. The lesson this past week was on forgiveness. He suggested I come home for a visit to ask you to forgive me for my bad behavior. So, I want to ask each of you to forgive me for scaring you and causing this stress in our family. Will you forgive me?" Dad asked as he looked at each of our faces.

"But, Dad," Sara said, "weren't you suffering from this condition, PTSD, and your mind was playing tricks on you?"

"I know you might think it was not my fault but this is something I really want and need to do. There is so much I've been learning about what it means to trust God.

"I hope you can see this is going to be the beginning of a new part of our family. I see now how important it is to bring God into the healing process, and the first step for me is to ask your forgiveness," Dad explained.

Mom spoke next and said, "Honey, we, too, have been learning how to turn to God when we have a need, and this is a great big one. I forgive you. I want you to know we are here for you and look forward to the day you can come home permanently. We love you so much." She jumped up and gave Dad a great big hug.

Sara and I looked at each other and we both jumped up, hugged Dad, and said at the same time, "We forgive you, too, Dad!"

After we all sat down again, Dad said, "There is something else I need to ask you before the birthday party begins."

"You are going to need a Bible for this

so each of you go get one, please," he stated confidently. Ever since we'd been attending church, Mom made sure we each had a Bible we liked.

We all ran to our bedrooms, found our Bibles, came back to the living room and sat down. He gave us each a sticky note with a Bible verse written on it and asked us to look up those verses and be ready to share. My note had John 3:16 on it.

Dad came and helped me look it up in the New Testament. Dad said, "Before you all read your verse out loud, I want to tell you a little story."

"The day I was arrested and brought down to the brig was the worst day of my life. Inside I was asking myself, 'Why did you do such a stupid thing?' My commanding officer asked that I have a 72-hour psych evaluation, so off I went to the hospital for a few days. When the psychiatrist wrote the report, he said I was suffering from severe Combat Trauma which is PTSD, and needed to spend time in recovery. They moved me into the dormitory at the Wounded Warrior Battalion. Chaplain Johnson came to visit me the day I moved in, and asked if we could get together three times a week and talk. Because I was so down, I thought, 'Why not? What have I got to lose?'

"It has been several months now, and we have been doing some major studying of God's Word.

"I know it has helped me in getting on the road to recovery from the stress I have been experiencing. So, with that said, I want to share some of the great

information I have been learning about what to do if I want God to help me get better.

"Jacob, would you read John 3:16 out loud, please?"

"Sure, Dad. It says, 'God so loved the world that He gave his only Son, so that everyone who believes in Him won't perish but will have eternal life.'"

"I realized," continued Dad, "I had never asked God to help me through any of my problems. I thought God was for sissies. One of the first things Chaplain Johnson showed me was that Jesus Christ came to Earth as a part of God's plan to take care of all the sins ever committed by every man, woman and child. He told me that just believing in God was not enough. I also had to believe in Jesus as God's Son and ask Him to come and live in my heart.

"It would be the first step in healing from PTSD. I was so-o-o-o ready to make things right and I saw that asking Jesus into my heart was a good thing so I prayed a simple prayer.

"What I want you three to know is that I want to make sure you have all prayed that prayer too."

Then Dad looked at Sara and Mom and asked, "Who has John 1:12 and 13 on their sticky note?"

Sara quickly raised her hand and read the verses out loud.

"'But those who did welcome Him, those who believed in His name, He authorized to become God's children, born not from blood nor from human desire or passion, but born from God.'"

I spoke up, "Dad, does that mean a man like you is a child again?"

"Good question, Jacob. I think it means no matter what age you are, we are all God's children once we become a part of His family of believers. Does that make sense?" Dad asked.

"The prayer I prayed went something like this:

> 'Dear God, I believe Jesus is Your Son. Thank You that Jesus died on the cross for the wrong things I have done. Please forgive me for doing wrong. I ask that Jesus will be with me and in me always. Help me to be the kind of person You want me to be. Thank You for answering my prayer. Amen'

"Have any of you said a prayer like that?" asked Dad.

Mom told Dad that we had been going to church with the Pooles ever since he had been arrested. "We have been trying to go every Sunday, but we have not really prayed a prayer like that in all that time," she told him.

"Guys, would you like to pray that prayer together?" We all nodded our heads and Dad asked us to stand in a circle and hold our hands. As he said each phrase of the prayer, he asked us to repeat the words. Afterward we opened our eyes and smiled and hugged each other. Then Dad told Mom to read her verse out loud. As she grabbed her Bible the rest of us sat down, ready to listen. Her verse was very short.

She said, "I am reading from Galatians 3:26, and it says, 'You are all God's children through faith in Christ Jesus.'"

Just then the doorbell rang several times, and Barney jumped up and ran to the front door, wagging his tail. It was time for the birthday party to begin! Inside my heart though, I felt even happier than I did when Dad stood at the door just a short time ago. I think our family is going to be better than it ever was.

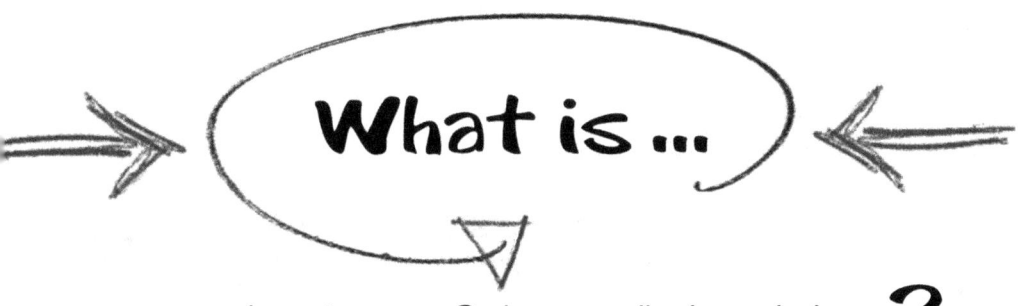

What is ...

so important about knowing God personally through Jesus?
(praying a prayer to ask Him to come into my heart)

Answer: The major reason that keeps people from knowing God personally is they don't know who God is and what He has done for us. He is patiently waiting for us to go to Him for help when we need it. He has had a plan for how to do that for a very long time. We have to be ready to turn to God but the way to know Him personally is through the gift of life that His Son, Jesus Christ, has made for us.

We are considered sinful but when we receive that gift by inviting Jesus into our hearts, and asking God to forgive us of all our sins, He will come into our hearts. When He does that, He gives us a clean heart.

Inviting Jesus into our hearts shows we have faith that our sins are forgiven, and that we will be made new. It also shows we trust God to do what He said He would do ... accept us into His family as a child of God ... no matter what age we are or what sins we have done.

What is...

the next step our family should take after we've prayed the prayer?

(What is expected of us?)

Answer: Spiritual growth results from trusting Jesus Christ. A life of faith from now on will give you what you need to grow in knowledge and understanding of the Christian life. Practice the following regularly:

- **G**o to God in prayer daily (John 15:7).

- **R**ead God's Word daily (Acts 17:11). A good place to start is the Gospel of John.

- **O**bey God moment by moment (John 14:21).

- **W**itness for Christ by your life and words (Matthew 4:19; John 15:8).

- **T**rust God for every detail of your life (1 Peter 5:7).

- **H**oly Spirit - Allow Him to control and help your daily life and witness (Galatians 5:16,25; Acts 1:8).

Galatians 3:11b says,
"The righteous man will live on the basis of faith."

God's Words

When I Need Understanding

"We know that God's Son has come and has given us understanding to know the One who is true. We are in the One who is true by being in his Son, Jesus Christ. This is the true God and eternal life."
~ 1 John 5:20

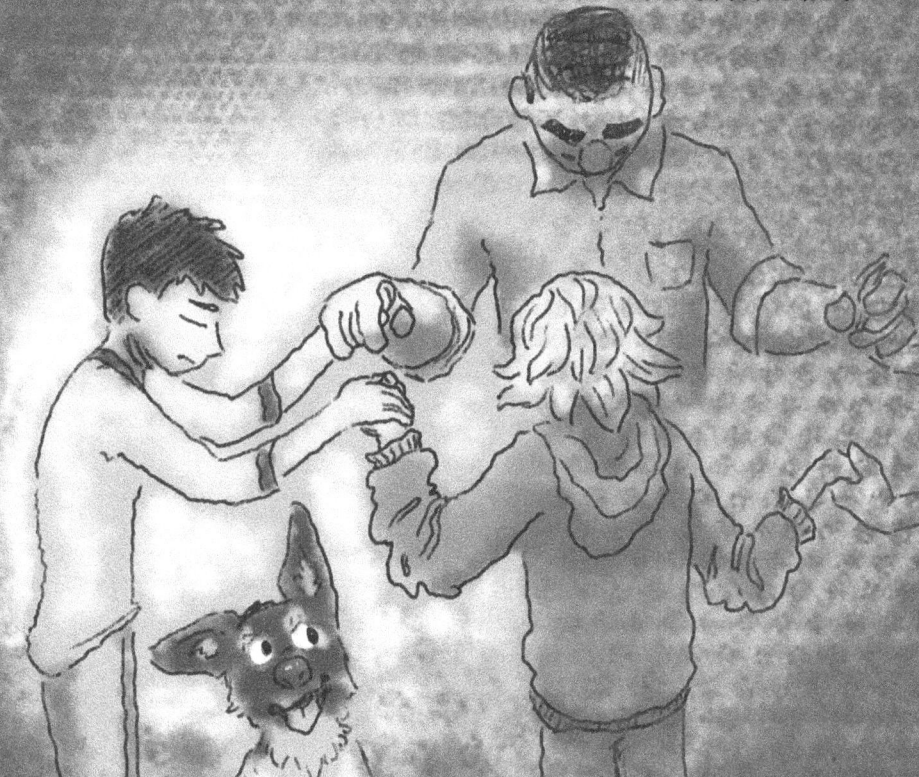

"Think about what I'm saying; the Lord will give you understanding about everything."
~ 2 Timothy 2:7

Discoveries

What Does God Use to Heal Someone with PTSD?

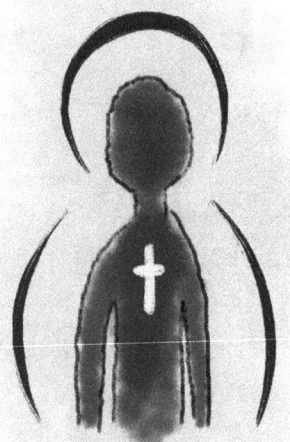

- **The Holy Spirit** - sent to reside within us, gives us power, comforts us, heals us, transforms us, helps us communicate with God and helps us to live a righteous and satisfying life

  The Three Distinct Persons Referred to as God:
  God the Father - John 6:27
  God the Son - John 20:26-28
  God the Holy Spirit - 1 Corinthians 3:16

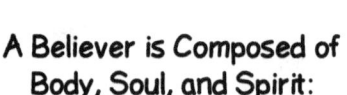

- **The Word of God -** given to us to provide the words of wisdom and information we need to use to live a life that deepens our relationship with God

A Believer is Composed of Body, Soul, and Spirit:

- **Our Body -** the physical body that each of us is born with, which we can use to honor God
- **Our Soul -** our will, intellect, understanding and emotions, which is nourished or fed by things like truth, beauty, love, knowledge and friendships
- **Our Spirit -** the part of us that relates to God, which is fed by the Word of God, the Bible

- **Prayer** - given to us as a way to communicate with God, Jesus and the Holy Spirit

The Purpose of Prayer

God loves to answer the requests we make of Him in prayer, but there is more to it. He is not there to act like a Santa Claus granting us a special gift to make us happy. Prayer is the communication link to God. Some of the benefits of prayer are healing, strength, power, knowing God's will for our lives, confession, daily spiritual food, keeping us from sinning, giving us peace and so much more.

- **The Christian Community** - given to us so we can be surrounded by people who love God, care for each other and worship God together

  1. We have friends who are understanding.
  2. We care for each other in time of need.
  3. We can be happy for each other when blessings come our way.
  4. We can fight loneliness because our friends are close by.
  5. We can encourage others when they are down.
  6. We can pray and study God's Word together.

- **Attitudes** - Our job is to keep our minds fixed on God and His ways by keeping godly attitudes, so He can accomplish His healing work in us.

  1. We will find **courage** in time of need.
  2. We will find **truth** as we continue to trust God.
  3. We will find **peace** as we remain thankful in all things.
  4. We will find **forgiveness** both in granting and receiving.
  5. We will find **joy** in sorrow only because God helps us.

POSITIVE ACTIVITIES

- Read a chapter in my Bible every day before doing my homework. Start with the Book of John.

- Use the journal book Mom gave me to study the Bible with the SPACE-Q plan. Study the chapter to see if there are things for me to learn, and make a chart to follow such as:

Date	Chap/Verses	S	P	A	C	E	Q

- **S**ins to confess - Review the list of possible wrong things I might do, found in Chapter 4.

- **P**romises to claim - "Through His honor and glory He has given us His precious and wonderful promises." 2 Peter 1:4

- **A**ctions to avoid - By studying God's Word, we learn how to live a happy life.

- **C**ommands to obey - We show love to God when we obey His commands.

- **E**xamples to follow - such as 1 Thessalonians 5:18, "Give thanks in every situation because this is God's will for you in Christ Jesus."

- **Q**uestions I need answered - Write down any questions that someone older can answer, such as a parent, a Sunday School teacher, a youth group leader, or camp counselor.

Jacob's Prayer

"Dear God, thank You for helping our family find You together. Thank You that my dad is getting better every day. Help us learn more about what it means to be a Christian military family. Continue to help everyone in my family heal from our wounds, especially my dad. Thank You for our future and the hope we have because of You. Amen"

 ## The Important Life Value is:

Patience
(definition: having the quality of waiting for the outcome, whatever that may be)

I want to wait for God's timing to heal my dad. I want to be known for having patience and not for getting angry when I am frustrated and confused.

signed, Jacob

Chapter 7
Story by Jenna

Tomorrow my dad will get home from his long deployment. Mom kept getting phone calls to say the arrival date was being pushed back to another time. It seems like this was the third call telling her of a different day. This has happened before so we should be used to it, but it is still hard when it keeps on changing.

"Jenna, do you want to run over to the church with me? I need to pick up a book a friend is lending me. We can also pick up your brother from karate practice and then go to the mall food court afterwards. What do you say?"

"That sounds good, Mom. I just have two more math problems and I'll be done with my homework," I said.

When we had finished the errands and walked into the mall, we saw that the reporter who had interviewed us for the TV news report a few days ago was in line at our favorite fast food restaurant. He greeted us with smiles and handshakes all around.

"Thanks so much for helping with my interview on the returning military story. You did such a great job. I appreciate how you spoke from the heart. I am sure it will help other families going through the same experiences. Off the record, I really don't know if I could do what you do over and over again when your husband and father go away so many times," the eager young reporter said as he looked at each of us.

Mom spoke up, "We've been in the military for many years now and we have learned to adapt to where we live and the schedule my husband has for his work. We know it comes with the job and try to do our part in accepting it all. I appreciate your kind words. By the way, my husband will be home tomorrow. Finally! We are so excited, especially Jenna and her brother."

When we picked up our order of food, the young reporter asked if we could all sit together. He was waiting for his wife to meet him in the food court. He said he had some more questions but these were for his own information.

"Of course you can join us," Mom said.

After we all sat down and started eating, our new friend looked at Mom and said, "When we did the interview the other day, you said your faith had a lot to do with how you deal with the multiple deployments your family has endured. What did you mean by that?"

I could not keep quiet any longer. "Mom, can I say something?"

"Yes, Jenna. Why don't you tell him what you have discovered about faith, and why it is so important to you."

"When I was in third grade, I was always afraid my dad was not going to come home from being overseas. I would cry a lot, and my mom told me about how much God loves me and knows all about my worries. She helped me understand that God wanted me to trust Him with everything. In the Bible, God explains all about His Son, Jesus, and I prayed a prayer to ask Him to come into my heart and help me not worry so much. He did!" I told him with a huge smile.

Mom said, "After Jenna asked for help, we got involved in a great church, and it has been a blessing to be surrounded by like-minded people who put all their trust in God and the Bible. We, as a family, are very involved in our church, and the activities they have for the kids and for us parents too.

"I have made some lifetime friends but, most of all, we have grown closer to God because of what we see, hear and do through our church. Do you and your wife go to a church anywhere?" Mom finally asked the young man.

"No, not really. I guess with my job and my wife finishing up her college degree, we don't really think about going to church because we are always so busy," the reporter confessed.

Mom said, "We'd love to invite you and your wife to go with us on Sunday. My husband will be home and you can meet him too. I know he'd love to meet you both."

Just then I heard someone call my name from a few tables away. "Hi, Jenna and Mrs. Poole!" It was Sara and her mom and brother. My brother waved at Jacob. We all went over to their table to say hello, and introductions and handshakes were made all around.

Suddenly, the young reporter waved at someone entering the mall food court. It must have been his wife because she waved back and gave him a big smile.

"Well, I have to go, but I have really enjoyed our talk, and I am interested in joining you on Sunday, along with my wife." He handed my mom a business card and told her to email the address and they would meet us there for the first service.

I heard him telling his wife when they were walking away, "Honey, I think we should be going to church on Sundays. These people have invited us to join them, and I think it would help us a lot. They are the family I interviewed for that military piece I was working on. What do you think?"

I could see her nodding her head yes, as she turned around to wave at us with a big smile.

What is...

missing from the young reporter's life because he does not go to church?

(Is it necessary to go to church to know God?)

Answer: God is ready to meet anyone anywhere, but a good church is a place where he can hear a talk that will help him understand what is found in the Bible. There is usually a good youth group leader who gives good talks that can help young people grow in the knowledge of their faith as well.

These talks are important because they help people understand how to live the Christian life. Jenna learned to have peace in her heart instead of being constantly worried about what would happen to her father when he was deployed. She and her family have learned what it means to have a personal relationship with God through Jesus Christ. It has given them a hope that keeps them trusting in God's ways, no matter what.

What is...

the benefit from taking time out of a busy schedule to go to church?

(What will be gained by going to church?)

Answer: Meeting with a group of people who all love God and want to learn more about Him is encouraging. It is a first step in adding a spiritual element to life. It is important to be friends with those who want to be involved in good actions, good attitudes, and good activities that bring them closer to God. Some of these activities are prayer, Bible study, youth group, serving others and so much more.

God's Words

When I Need to Know God

"Those who God
decided in
advance would
be conformed to
His Son,
He also called.
Those whom
He called,
He also made
righteous.
Those whom
He made righteous,
He also glorified."
~ Romans 8:30

"God so loved the world that
He gave His only Son, so that everyone who
believes in Him won't perish but will have
eternal life."
~ John 3:16

Discoveries

Note: There are times when feelings will get in the way. It takes time and many factors to come together in order to mature as a Christian. When you experience some of the negative activities listed below, get ready to change a habit or two, so you can be on the right track. Remember the importance of following God's ways at home, at school, at church, at the mall, at sporting practices and games, at the park playing with friends, and everywhere you go. Choose to do the right thing based on what you learn in the Bible.

Some Negative Activities to Avoid

- Feeling sorry for yourself
- Complaining
- Sitting around doing nothing
- Eating unhealthy food
- Not cleaning your room regularly
- Making excuses for not going to church
- Not studying God's Word
- Not praying
- Not saying, "I'm sorry," when you should
- Not obeying your parents right away

POSITIVE ACTIVITIES

- Read good books written by and for Christians.
- Listen to uplifting music.
- Serve as a volunteer in the church childcare.
- Help a neighbor do yardwork while their dad is away.
- Bake cookies to bring to neighbors' families ... just because.
- Spend time with a friend in prayer.
- Volunteer to go with the youth group on a mission trip.
- Spend regular time studying God's Word.
- Take up a sport or new exercise program.
- Do unexpected chores to surprise Mom and Dad without being asked.

Jenna's Prayer

"Dear God, thank You for how You helped me not to worry so much. I pray the reporter and his wife find what they are looking for at church. Lead them to Your ways, Lord. Help me to be the kind of person who is more positive than negative. Amen"

 ## The Important Life Value is:

Understanding
(definition: to comprehend and perceive the meaning of a subject matter)

I desire to have a greater understanding of the Christian life. I want to be able to easily explain to someone why I have faith.

signed, Jenna

How Can Friends Help?

Chapter 8

Story by Jacob

Since Jenna's dad came home from his deployment a month ago, our families have been doing all kinds of fun things together. It has been great. Dad has been coming to stay at home on weekends, and we have all been going to church together. What a difference it has made in all of our lives. I've never seen everyone so happy all at the same time. Dad has been helping me learn how to be a Little League catcher on Saturday and Sunday afternoons. He used to play baseball in college, and seems to still know his stuff.

We have our first game of the season this afternoon, and Dad promised he would come to watch me play. I can't wait to show him what I can do.

"Batter-up," the umpire yelled as he swept the home plate base clean of sand and dirt. The first batter walked up to the base and waited for the pitch. I've been working with the boy who is pitching for our team, and he is usually pretty good at getting the ball close to where I can catch it.

"Strike one," the ump yelled.

That was an easy one to catch. After throwing the ball back to the pitcher, I looked over at the bleachers where the parents were sitting and could not see my dad.

"Oh, well," I thought.

The game went on to the 5th inning and our team was ahead by one point. The coach was very happy with our playing and told us over and over, "Good job, guys, you are keeping your eyes on the ball. Let's finish this inning with a win. You can do it."

It was my turn to bat and as I looked over the crowd while getting into position, I finally saw my dad sitting in the last row. He waved at me and I nodded and smiled real big. I was so determined to get a good hit while Dad was watching so I could hear him say, "Great job, Jacob!"

The first two balls whizzed by me and it was two strikes just like that. It was now or never for me to get a good hit. After three straight balls, I now had a full count. The next pitch nicked my bat and flew off to the side.

"Oh my gosh," I thought, "that was close! I have to remember to keep my eyes on the ball and not look at the scoreboard."

As the pitch came at me, I heard my dad yelling from the grandstands, "Make it count, son!"

Just then, I connected with the ball. It went far into left field where no player was standing or could catch it.

As I hustled around the bases, I could hear the crowd clapping and shouting my name. The left fielder threw the ball to the third base but I was already running towards home plate.

Wow! I made it with a slide and scored a run. What a good feeling that was.

When Dad, Mom and Sara came to congratulate our team for winning the game, Dad grabbed me and gave me a big hug. "You were great, Jacob! Not only did you do a great job of catching but hitting too. I'm so proud of you!"

Some of the other guys on the team came and congratulated me as we were all walking from the field to the parking lot.

When we got home and cleaned up for dinner, Dad told us all to come into the living room. He had something to talk to us about.

One by one, we made it to the living room, wondering what Dad was going to say.

"It has been six months since I came home from my last deployment. Thank you so much for helping me get through this unexpected result of being in the war zone overseas. I never saw it coming but to be honest, I think we are all closer and have a new outlook on life. I am especially excited with how Chaplain Johnson helped me see my need for trusting in God. There is still so much to learn, and I know we would have been in a different place without the help of others in our lives."

Mom started to cry, but I think it was happy tears. She didn't say anything but just stood up and walked over to hug Dad.

We all got up then and rushed Dad with some more big hugs. Barney always loves to get into the middle of this kind of activity and was wagging his tail very fast, jumping up to be included in the hugs.

After we sat down again, Dad said, "My commanding officer said after a few evaluations and some paperwork, I can report to my regular duty again. I can also come home to live full time."
"That is so cool, Dad, then we can play catch every day when you come home from work," I said excitedly,
"I'll get even better than I am right now. Yay!!"

What is...

expected of a family who wants to help another family dealing with combat trauma?

(becoming a "Bridge to Healing" family or "Battle Buddies")

Answer: God desires us to practice the following actions as we help others. After each verse, list an activity you can think of to help someone.

- "We who are powerful need to be patient with the weakness of those who don't have power, and not please ourselves."
  Romans 15:1

  _____

  _____

- "Carry each other's burdens and so you will fulfill the law of Christ." *Galatians 6:2*

  _____

  _____

- "Conduct yourselves with all humility, gentleness, and patience. Accept each other with love." *Ephesians 4:2*

  _____

  _____

- "Be kind, compassionate, and forgiving to each other, in the same way God forgave you in Christ." *Ephesians 4:32*

  _____

  _____

- "For this reason, confess your sins to each other and pray for each other so that you may be healed. The prayer of the righteous person is powerful in what it can achieve."
  James 5:16

  _____

  _____

What is ... a list of some practical ideas of how to help?

(ways to come alongside each member of a family dealing with combat trauma)

Answer:

- **Be eager to help whenever needed** - babysitting, dog-walking, giving rides
- **Be ready to work hard if need be** - cooking meals, yardwork
- **Be a good listener** - phone, email, face to face
- **Be on the lookout for ways to reach out** - offer to take kids to school, ride bikes and play together
- **Be truthful when needed** - pay sincere compliments, give biblical answers to hard questions
- **Be an encourager** - make, bake and take a favorite food to share; send notes of hope
- **Be a prayer warrior** - pray in person, keep a prayer journal for specific daily prayer

God's Words

When I Need to be Sensitive to Others

"Encourage each other every day... so none of you become insensitive to God because of sin's deception."

~ Hebrews 3:13

"Two are better than one because they have a good return for their hard work."

~ Ecclesiastes 4:9

Discoveries

Facts to know about PTSD/Combat Trauma

Note: Even when PTSD/Combat Trauma has not affected someone close to you, it is important to understand what other families are experiencing because of the condition.

- Those serving in a war zone are experiencing extremely difficult events.
- Reactions to the war zone can be experienced physically, mentally, emotionally and spiritually.
- There are mild to severe reactions, and some take months to show up.
- Severe reactions may include isolation, loss of joy in life, nightmares, reliving the war, not sleeping.
- Having combat trauma does not mean people are weak, crazy or cowardly.
- The wounds of combat trauma need to be healed just like a broken arm needs healing.
- Sometimes drugs and alcohol are used to "forget" the war zone.
- A wound of the mind needs a lot of patience, love and care from family members.
- Speaking to a pastor and studying the Word of God will help bring healing for wounds of the soul.
- Physical wounds can be seen, but wounds of the mind are hard to detect.

POSITIVE ACTIVITIES

Writing Assignment

1. Write a short essay on "MY HERO." (Use your dad as the hero.)
2. Include positive characteristics and why they count.
3. Include a very specific time or incident telling how your dad was a hero to you.
4. Include future adventures you'd like to experience with your hero.
5. Use your best handwriting to make a final copy on nice paper.
6. Be sure to sign and date your essay.
7. Frame your "MY HERO" piece, wrap it up and give it to your dad as a special gift.

Jacob's Prayer

> "God, thank You for my father. Thank You for who he is and what he has accomplished in his life. Help me be the kind of son who encourages him, no matter what. Help me be sensitive to his feelings. Thank You for the healing You have done in his life. I am so grateful!! Amen"

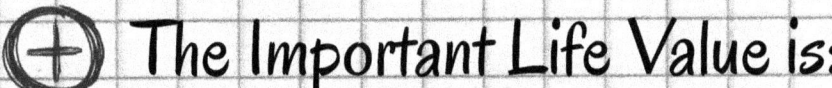
⊕ The Important Life Value is:

Humility
(definition: valuing others more than myself)

I desire to put others first, especially my dad. When he comes home to live at our house again, I want all of us to be happy. I want to be a positive influence.

signed, Jacob

Am I God's Child?

Chapter 9
Story by Sara

I am so super excited today. It was the best breakfast news I've heard in a long time. Dad gets to move back home on Saturday. YAY!! I can't wait to tell Jenna when the bus picks us up for our twenty-minute ride to school.

While we were standing in line to enter the bus, I whispered into Jenna's ear, "Dad is moving back home on Saturday."

Jenna turned around with a huge smile and said, "Oh, Sara that is so cool! Are you going to have a party to celebrate?"

"Not sure what Mom has planned, but we will be in church on Sunday morning. I know that much," I replied.

After the bus dropped us off at school, I saw a group of girls pointing at me and giggling. It was a surprise to see those girls acting that way. I didn't like the way they kept staring and laughing. It made me feel uncomfortable. While the teacher in math class was explaining a problem on the board, I felt a tap on my shoulder. When I looked around, the boy sitting behind me handed me a note. After looking to make sure the teacher did not see, I opened and read what was written on the note.

> Too bad your dad had to go to jail. ^_^
> Guess he has been a bad boy.
> Sure hope you don't have to go to jail too!!!!!!!! O_O

I quickly shoved the note into my backpack and looked straight ahead. Somehow, I knew that note came from one of those girls staring at me this morning. I wonder who told them about my dad and the police.

For the rest of the day at school, I couldn't stop thinking about that mean note. I kept taking it out when I thought no one was looking to see if I could figure out whose handwriting it was. Didn't have any luck in that regard.

After school, I must have been acting strangely because Mom noticed something was not right and she asked me, "Sara, did you have a bad day at school or what? You look like it is the end of the world!"

I grabbed my backpack, pulled out the note and showed it to her. As she read the words, the look on her face changed and she came to give me a big hug.

"Sweetheart, you realize the person who wrote this does not know the real story about what happened. They still should not have given it to you, but you must not hold a grudge against them. People who do this kind of bullying are usually hurting themselves in some way. They are just trying to make themselves feel better by making another person feel worse than they feel. Have you been able to guess who did it?" asked Mom.

"No, not really. But today, when Jenna and I were walking to the building after getting off the bus, I saw a group of girls staring and laughing while pointing their fingers at me. I am sure it is one of them. It made me feel so terrible inside, I just wanted to run and hide. After I read the note, I wanted to cry," I confessed.

Mom told me to sit down at the kitchen counter and she would be right back. When she returned, she had her Bible with her and sat down next to me.

"One of the things I have been learning in the women's Bible study I go to at church is what I am worth in God's eyes. Let's take a peek together at some verses and then you tell me how you feel after we talk about them," she said as she opened her Bible.

She pointed to some verses in Ephesians and asked me to read them out loud. It said, "You are saved by God's grace because of your faith. This salvation is God's gift. It's not something you possessed. It's not something you did that you can be proud of. Instead, we are God's accomplishment, created in Christ Jesus to do good things. God planned for these good things to be the way that we live our lives."

"Sara, remember when we prayed to invite Jesus into our lives?" Mom asked.

I silently nodded my reply.

"The experience we have had with Dad is no mistake. God has been using it in all of our lives in different ways. He is causing all of us to reach out to Him for understanding, forgiveness, and most of all, to make us better people. What has happened with the mean note gives you a chance to show forgiveness to that group of girls. It may be they don't have any knowledge about Post-Traumatic Stress Disorder," Mom said.

She continued, "They are obviously not showing good judgment in how they are treating you. I think they need a good dose of education on the subject. I know Dad would agree with me if you went to your teacher at school and asked if you could read your English report out loud to the whole school. The writing project you and Jenna did would be perfect. You can also tell the class how this condition has affected our family. What do you think?" she asked at the end.

"Mom, I am really glad to have you as my mom. I like being a Christian, and our whole family seems so much happier since this has happened to us. I will talk to my teacher tomorrow and see what he says. I like, too, that Dad gets to come home to live on Saturday. I can't wait to spend more time with him. God has really helped us so much!"

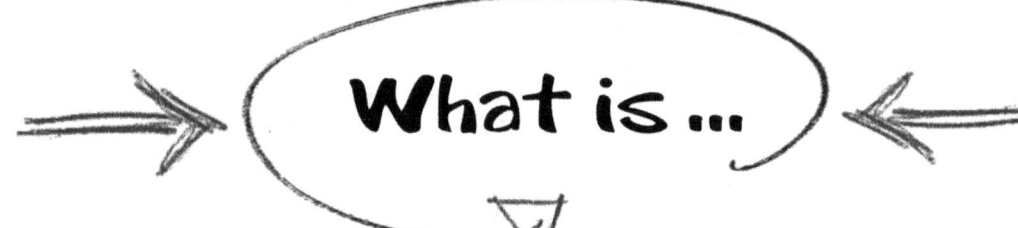

What is...

important to know about what God thinks about me?

(My identity as a Christian helps me deal with negative experiences in life.)

Answer:

- In God's eyes, you hold an important position as His child for eternity.

- He has called you to be a light to those around you who don't know about Him.

- You are being trained and qualified for leadership now and in the future.

- Wounds in life will happen, but it is how you respond to them that is important.

- You have a job to do as a Christian ... to show love to one another.

What is...

important to know about Satan's tricks and deceptions?

(Satan is God's enemy and is a Christian's enemy too!)

Answer: Just as God has a plan to help you, Satan has a plan to destroy you. It is not good to be ignorant of how Satan plays his games. No matter how old a person is, how wealthy a person is, or how smart a person is, Satan tries to make life miserable for everyone. He especially likes to deceive Christians, so they will turn their backs on God. Get to know Satan's lies!! Put a checkmark next to the lies you have believed before.

____ Lie Number **1:**   You are not cared for.

____ Lie Number **2:**   You are unimportant.

____ Lie Number **3:**   You can't be trusted.

____ Lie Number **4:**   You're not good enough.

____ Lie Number **5:**   You're such a loser.

____ Lie Number **6:**   You are weak.

____ Lie Number **7:**   You are worthless.

____ Lie Number **8:**   You are not wanted.

God's Words

When I Feel Weak

"I can endure all these things through the power of the One who gives me strength."

~ Philippians 4:13

"Let's not get tired of doing good, because in time we'll have a harvest if we don't give up."

~ Galatians 6:9

Discoveries

Complete the sentence or answer the question to discover who you are in Christ (look for clues in the verses).

- You were known, loved and chosen by God how long ago?
  _____

  "God chose us in Christ to be holy and blameless in God's presence before the creation of the world." Ephesians 1:4

- Since you have received Christ, you have rightly been named as what?
  _____

  "But those who did welcome Him, those who believed in His name, He authorized to become God's children." John 1:12

- What does God think about your sins and lawless behavior?
  _____

  "And I won't remember their sins and their lawless behavior anymore." Hebrews 10:17

- When we draw near to God's throne, we experience _____ and _____.

  "Finally, let's draw near to the throne of favor with confidence so that we can receive mercy and find grace when we need help." Hebrews 4:16

- What kind of spirit has God given us?
  _____

  "God didn't give us a spirit that is timid but one that is powerful, loving and self-controlled." 2 Timothy 1:7

- Fill in the blanks: _____ lives in me and I live this life by _____.

  "I have been crucified with Christ and I no longer live, but Christ lives in me. And the life that I now live in my body, I live by faith, indeed, by the faithfulness of God's Son, who loved me and gave Himself for me." Galatians 2:20

Answers: before the creation of the world; God's children; won't remember; mercy, grace; powerful, loving and self-controlled; Christ; faith

POSITIVE ACTIVITIES

- Make a nice WELCOME HOME sign for Dad's return home.
- Ask teacher to help with best idea of how to share with students about PTSD.
- Invite all girls from class over for a fun party.
- Say something nice to a new person every day.
- Ask Mom if she and I can go bike riding today after school.
- Take the negative action of the note and make it into a positive action.
- Make a page in my journal to write why I make a good friend.
- Recognize the enemy's lies and tell him to get lost! ("Go away, Satan! Get lost! Leave and don't come back!")

Sara's Prayer

"Dear God, thank You that I am Your child. Help me be a positive influence to everyone I know. Help me be a person who loves instead of someone who wants revenge. Help me be a person who wants to always do the right thing. Thank You for giving me a Christian family. Thank You for helping me every day and night. Amen!"

⊕ The Important Life Value is:

Thankfulness
(definition: having a feeling of appreciation and gratefulness)

I want to be thankful for all things that happen in my life. I thank God even for the ignorance of girls who tried to make me mad and sad. I desire to be a better person than that and want to bring a positive attitude instead.

signed, Sara

Chapter 10
Story by Jenna

It has been the best month of my life. Dad came home from this last deployment and is doing great. I was really wondering how that would be because of what happened to Sara's dad. I asked myself in the days before he arrived home again: Will my dad have PTSD? Will he not be the same Dad I have known all my life? I am so very happy he seems to be just fine.

"Is Dad home from work yet, Mom?" I yelled from my bedroom.

He and I were going on a double date with Sara and her dad tonight. I didn't want him to be late and I was almost ready to go. We were planning to eat at our favorite restaurant and then go see a movie together. I couldn't wait!

Just then a familiar voice called out from the kitchen, "Is my date ready?"

"I'll be right there," I said as I grabbed a jacket and my cell phone. We were on our way to a fun night. It was so cool to see the changes in Sara's dad. He seemed like an even better person than before he left to go on the last overseas trip. At the restaurant, we were all laughing because a little boy at the next table was making faces at us.

Sara's dad suddenly became a bit serious when he said, "Girls, there is something I want to discuss with you both. Rich and I have been talking lately about a very important subject. We feel you both are old enough to understand what I am about to say."

I looked at Dad and he smiled back, while nodding his head up and down.

"Since I have become a Christian, I have been so grateful to Chaplain Johnson because he has been teaching me about who the real enemy is in life," Sara's dad said.

He went on to say, "We are trained to know who the enemies in the war zone are and how to deal with them. I didn't realize there is even a more dangerous enemy out there who loves to be deceitful. He is always looking for ways to attack all people of all races and of all ages. There are many names for him in the Bible but I'm sure you have heard the name Satan."

Sara and I said, "Yes!" at the same time rather loudly, which made us all laugh.

Sara's dad continued speaking with some emotion, "When I came back from the war zone with some wounds of the heart because of what happened over there, I was at a weak spot.

"It did not occur to me that I had changed but now as I look back, I can see how my emotions were all screwed up.

"I needed some help but did not want to admit it. When I had the gun incident, I was at my lowest level of coping. I don't even know what triggered the reaction I had, but I do know Satan loved every minute of it," he explained.

"Chaplain Johnson shared a Bible verse that has helped me so much," he said as he took a small piece of paper from his wallet. "I carry it around to remind me who the real enemy is in this world." He read, "'We aren't fighting against human enemies but against rulers, authorities, forces of cosmic darkness, and spiritual powers of evil in the heavens.' That's in Ephesians 6:12."

My dad chimed in, "The devil, or Satan as he is called, has figured out a battle plan to disrupt our lives. He uses deceit to fool people so they turn against God. He loves it when they turn against each other whether it is family members, race against race, or nations against nations. He loves to confuse whenever he can, however he can."

I asked, "Is Satan causing the wars you go fight in?"

Dad explained, "A lot of what goes on when people fight each other is caused by Satan trying to cause problems. What do you think it would be like, though, if everyone tried to follow God's ways? Our world would be a totally different place. I might not be in the military but have some other kind of career.

"Because of the sin that started with Adam and Eve, we are going to have these kinds of battles in the world. God gives lots of instruction in the Bible of how to fight our Number One Enemy. It is important to keep on studying what it says in there. Right, girls?"

Sara said, as she looked at her cell phone, "I'm so glad we are all on God's side now! Hey! We should be getting over to the theater soon. The movie starts in 15 minutes!"

Later that evening, as I crawled into bed, my thoughts were about the double-date I'd had with my dad and friends. The dinner was great! The movie was fun! But, when our dads explained how the enemy works, I found it to be very interesting. I am going to study more about how to do battle with him, I want to be ready!

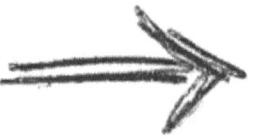 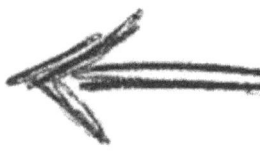

What is...

something to know about Satan that would be helpful to me?

(need to know how to fight the battle)

Answer:
- Satan looks for ways to keep us from loving and obeying God.
- Satan is deceitful and hides around every corner, waiting for us to trip up.
- Satan fills our head with lies, waiting for us to believe them.
- Satan works hard to keep people from growing in their knowledge of God.

Who is he?

What is...

something I can do to fight against the world's Number One Enemy?

(need to have a battle plan)

Answer: It is important to know how to fight the enemy. The full armor of God found in Ephesians 6:13-17 is a good place to read. Copy those verses on a 3x5 card and put it up in your room where you see it every day. Memorize it and be ready to use each part of the armor when needed.

- Belt of **Truth** around your waist
- **Justice** as your breastplate
- Shoes on your feet ready to spread the Good News of **Peace**
- Shield of **Faith**
- Helmet of **Salvation**
- Sword of the Spirit ~ **God's Word**

God's Words

When I Need Strength

"You've given me the shield of Your salvation; Your strong hand has supported me; Your help has made me great."

~ Psalm 18:35

"Finally, be strengthened by the Lord and His powerful strength. Put on God's armor so that you can make a stand against the tricks of the devil."

~ Ephesians 6:10,11

Discoveries
Drawing the Battle Lines with Prayers

- **Example of a prayer for spiritual victory:**

"Dear Lord, thank You that through Jesus' death on the cross, I have moment-by-moment cleansing from sin. Thank You that it does not matter how old I am; You want me to call upon Your power at any time. Thank You that the work on the cross Jesus did means Satan's work amounts to nothing. I know I can accomplish much and conquer all things because You love me. I want to give You this prayer in the name of the Lord Jesus with thanksgiving. Amen"

- **Example of a prayer for my family:**

"Dear Lord, thank You for my wonderful family. Thank You that my mom and dad love each other and love me and my brother. I want to be a good person and want to trust You with our relationships. May You give us peace when there is trouble. May You give us compassion when there is conflict. And may You give us Your eyes so we see when we have done something wrong and need to ask forgiveness. Also help us see when Satan is tricking us. Amen"

- **Example of a prayer for someone who has PTSD symptoms:**

"Dear Lord, make the hearts of those suffering stronger each day. Help their eyes see that You are the best refuge and strength during times of weakness. Help people see You are the reason to hope, to trust, to communicate, and to wait patiently for the healing to take place. I pray those suffering will cry out for the best kind of help You can give. Amen"

POSITIVE ACTIVITIES

- Invite Sara and her brother over to spend the night.
- Remember to pray every night for my family and Sara's family.
- Draw a picture to show me wearing the **Armor of God.**
- Ask Mom and Dad if our whole family can volunteer together somewhere.
- Volunteer to be a tutor during math class, my favorite subject.
- Learn more about the **Armor of God** and teach it to other young people.
- Write a **"Thankfulness"** letter to all my loved ones.

Jenna's Prayer

> "Dear God, thank You for all of the good instructions in the Bible to help me be a better person. Thank You for my family. Help us to reach out to others all around us who are hurting. Keep my eyes open to Satan's tricks of deceit, lies and dishonesty. Help me know the difference between right and wrong my whole life. Amen"

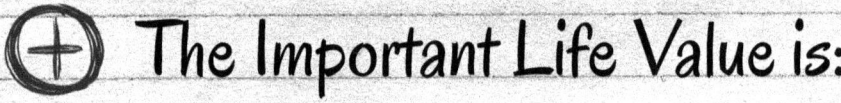 **The Important Life Value is:**

Trust
(definition: confident expectation of something)

I want to be one who trusts God all the time. I want to pursue all I can learn in the Bible about being a person others can trust because I am trustworthy. I want to be someone who keeps my path straight and true to Jesus.

signed, Jenna

How Can I Help My Mom and Dad?

Dad has been home now for six weeks and we ha[ve]
been doing so much better lately. At first it w[as a]
bit awkward because not only had he been livin[g in]
the Wounded Warrior Battalion dormitory for si[x months]
but he had also been deployed for eight mont[hs before]
that. Jacob and I know a lot more about PTSD [than we]
did several months ago. We have seen that wo[rking]
 [...] on this problem has helped all o[f us]

Chapter 11
Story by Sara

"Dad has been home now for six weeks and we have been doing so much better lately. At first it was a bit awkward because not only had he been living at the Wounded Warrior Battalion dormitory for six months, but he had also been deployed for eight months before that. Jacob and I know a lot more about PTSD than we did several months ago. We have seen working as a family on this problem has helped all of us."

I wrote these words in today's entry for a journal-writing project from school. Even though school is out for the summer months, I have not stopped writing in my journal. As soon as I was done writing and closed the journal, I heard Mom calling my name. "Sara, could you come in the kitchen, please?"

As I entered the doorway to the kitchen, I saw a lady and man sitting at the table drinking coffee. They all had very happy looks on their faces.

"Chaplain and Mrs. Johnson, this is my daughter, Sara," said Mom. As they reached out to me, she indicated that I shake their hands. Then I sat down at the table with them.

"Chaplain Johnson and his wife have been explaining an idea they have had because of what our family has experienced with Dad's PTSD problem. He would like to see if our family would share the story with all of those who attend the chapel services. He wants each one of us to say something and will give us a basic outline. We are to talk about what each of us felt as we went through this time in our lives. What do you think?" asked Mom as she looked at me.

Since Jenna and I had written about PTSD, and the teacher had let us share our findings with the whole school, I knew this would not be so hard. After all, I thought, I probably know more abouWt the topic than most adults, who don't even know what the words are for the PTSD letters. "Yeah, I think that would be really good to do. Have you talked to Jacob yet?" I asked.

"I will tell him about it after baseball practice. He will be home at six o'clock. Dad really wants to do this, and I think it would be good for others to see how God played an important role in guiding us down the path to healing for all of us."

Chaplain Johnson spoke up, "We are thinking of having you all share at the service in three weeks. Does that give you enough time to prepare?"

I looked at Mom to see what she would say. "It sounds reasonable to me. I'm sure my husband will say that is okay since you have already spoken with him about this opportunity. I'll get back to you if there is any change," Mom said.

After our guests left, Mom came over and gave me a big hug and said, "I am so proud of you and how you have behaved during this test our family has had. Dad really loves being in the military, but I know he loves his family even more. He has changed so much for the better. I think it is crucial to let other families know about the progress we have made."

I looked into my mom's eyes and saw some tears coming but she smiled a great big smile and said, "Who knows? We may help other people who are suffering, but have not gone for help yet. They don't realize God has a plan to help them, if they are willing to let Him help. When

Dad gets home after picking up Jacob from practice, we'll sit down and plan what we should share with everyone. We can also ask God to give us the right words to say so they touch deep down inside those who are hurting."

After a great Mexican food dinner, we put the leftovers in the fridge and cleaned up the kitchen. Dad stuck his head around the corner and said, "Family meeting at the patio table in five minutes. Bring some paper and something to write with, and we'll get started on our family sharing project."

When we were all settled in our places at the table, Dad began by saying, "The first thing we need to do is pray."

When we had all closed our eyes and bowed our heads, he said, "God, we want You to help us with the right words to say so we can help others who may be suffering from PTSD. Most of all we want to give You the honor You deserve because of how You changed our family. We thank You for this opportunity and want to speak only words that give hope. And all of God's people said, 'Amen.'"

We all piped in and said, "Amen!" as we opened our eyes, ready to make a difference in someone's life.

What is...

the most important fact that each member of Sara's family should share with folks?

(the message that will speak into the needs of the men, women and children who still need to ask for help)

Answer:

Dad: He wants to focus on who the real enemy in life is and share how Satan used the war zone as a tool to get him to go off the deep end. He wants to tell how God intervened in his life and brought him from the trauma of war to the healing from the wounds of war.

Mom: She wants to tell how God brought friends into her life who led her on a journey of hope. Asking God to help her family get through the fear, uncertainty and feeling of hopelessness brought her comfort.

Sara: She wants to let other young people know about her experience with the bullying students at school. They were ignorant about what really was happening in her dad's life. She wants to let them know how God played a role in helping her understand how to react.

Jacob: He wants to read the story he wrote about his dad called, "My Hero." Even though his father behaved in some unusual ways, he wants everyone to know he is still his hero.

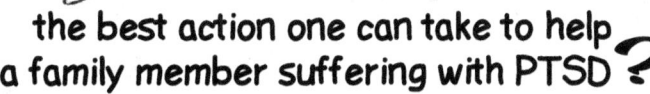

What is ... the best action one can take to help a family member suffering with PTSD?

(ways to help in the healing process)

Answer:

- Do what one can to get tasks done around the house without complaining.

- Be ready to be a good **listener**, an **encourager** and remain calm at all times.

- **Pray** through difficult times both with those who are hurting and for them (Philippians 4:6,7).

- Focus on the expression of feelings (for example: yelling) and not judge the characteristics shown (for example: seems to be angry).

- Think of unexpected ways to show **kindness**.

- Show **understanding** of the process that may seem slow (even if you don't understand).

- Do not give insults, as the tongue proves to be a contamination if not disciplined (1 Peter 3:9,10).

- Have some structured question and answer times to practice **good communication skills.** (See the "Discoveries" section of this chapter.)

- Be aware of what not to say, such as: "There's nothing wrong with you, I don't see any bandage!" or "Get over it!" or "You're no fun anymore!" or "Why can't we go to Disneyland or someplace fun anymore?"

- Instead of going out to eat, get take-out foods from favorite restaurants once a week.

God's Words
When I Need Courage

"All you who wait for the Lord, be strong and let your heart take courage."

~ Psalm 31:24

"It is my expectation and hope that I won't be put to shame in anything. Rather, I hope with daring courage that Christ's greatness will be seen in my body, now as always, whether I live or die."

~ Philippians 1:20

Discoveries
Questions and Answers for Good Communication Skills

Note: A suggestion is to write each question on a small piece of paper. Fold all the question papers and place in a container of some kind such as a small basket, box or bag. Draw out one question at a time and take turns answering. Allow each member of the family to choose at least one question.

1. What was the hardest thing for you during the time we were apart?
2. What kinds of letters did you like to get?
3. What were you most looking forward to after the deployment was over?

4. Who gave you the best kind of support during the deployment? After the deployment?
5. What is one memory of our family that you thought a lot about?
6. What happened after the deployment that disappointed you?
7. What happened after the deployment that surprised you?
8. What happened after the deployment that made you sad?
9. What happened after the deployment that made you happy?
10. What is something you get annoyed at that makes it difficult for you?
11. What is one big dream you have for the future?
12. What did you think about God during the deployment?
13. What is one thing you don't understand about things of the Bible?
14. What is one thing you think should be changed in our family schedule?
15. What do you like to do for fun?

POSITIVE ACTIVITIES

- Suggest the family go bike riding together.
- Suggest the family read a book together.
- Suggest the family invite a neighboring family over for a BBQ.
- Offer to do everyone's laundry for the week.
- Offer to be a teacher's aide in one of the Sunday School classes.
- Offer to babysit so Jenna's parents and your parents can have a double date.
- Make Dad's favorite dessert and surprise him with it.
- Make an **I Love You Because ...** poster to put up as a surprise for Dad.
- Make an 8 1/2 X 11 collage of family photos with a border for Dad to take to work.

Sara's Prayer

> "Dear God, thank You so much for where our family is headed now and in the future. Help each one of us do our best when we speak in the chapel. Bring just the right families there who would love to hear our messages of healing. You are the best!! Amen"

 **The Important Life Value is:**

Courage
(definition: being able to face difficulties without fear)

I desire to be used by God in helping others know there is help from Him for PTSD problems. I want to share from my heart how God heals a whole family and there is hope for everyone.

signed, Sara

106

How Can We Help Others Our Age?

Chapter 12
Story by Sara

Jacob and I sat on the floor in the living room talking about our invitation to speak at chapel in a couple of weeks. "What are you going to say, Sara?" asked Jacob. Mom heard Jacob's question, as she came into the living room.

"I just got off the phone with the young reporter who interviewed Jenna's mom for a TV segment. He wants to tape our family speaking at the chapel service," said Mom as she sat down on the couch. "I think we need to have a family meeting and discuss what to say with more purpose in mind, since more people will be hearing our messages. What do you think about that?" she asked.

"Wow, Mom, that is so cool," Jacob said excitedly.

"Tonight after dinner, let's have a practice session; so come prepared with what you have so far." Barney came over and sat down next to us, looking at Jacob and me tilting his head back and forth with a look of curiosity.

That night we all sat around the dinner table with great anticipation about how we were going to do this family-sharing thing. I wasn't scared at all because I knew what we had to say could change someone's life. It was important to say the right thing and not point fingers at anyone

"The way I see it," Dad started out, "we should start at the gun incident. Sara, you could tell a little about how that affected you. Make sure you talk about how you felt when you got off the bus and saw my truck in the driveway. Tell what you saw and heard and how that made you feel." I nodded my head up and down.

"Honey," he said to Mom, "tell about some of the behaviors you were noticing and why we were arguing when I pulled out the gun." She nodded yes.

"I'm going to tell about how I knew something was not right when I got back from overseas, but I didn't believe anything was wrong, so I ignored it. I have learned so much about this affliction that many deny or laugh off. It isn't good for them to do that," Dad said sadly.

"Jacob, my boy, I love the 'My Hero' story that you wrote and put into a frame for me. I look at it and read it almost every day while I'm sitting at my desk at work. Are you up for reading that to everyone after we three have said our part?" Dad asked, as he ruffled up Jacob's hair. "I think it would make a powerful conclusion to our sharing time."

"I know I can do it, Dad," Jacob said.

"Good, let's meet again in a few days and see what everyone has written down. We'll practice so there won't be any surprises," Dad said with a grin.

Later that week, we gathered again around the dinner table with our notes laid out in front of us. Since learning how to do research in English class, I had even done some research on the Internet about how PTSD affects kids when someone in their family is suffering with it. I couldn't wait to share what I'd found out. I had an idea of how Jacob and I could tell the people how kids can be hurt by the actions of someone who does not believe they have PTSD. When we were done timing our practiced speeches, we were all happy with the results.

 # What is...

the best way to inform children about some of the symptoms they see in their parent?

(help them realize there is a wound that is inside the mind and heart)

Answer:

- Ask God to help give you wisdom (James 1:5).
- Ask for spiritual help from a chaplain, pastor or counselor.
- When a suffering parent is re-experiencing sad or violent events, the healthy parent should reassure the children that they are still loved and that this is not the children's fault.
- When a suffering parent is emotionally distant, the healthy parent should reassure the children that their wounded parent is in the process of healing and will get better soon.
- When a suffering parent is overly angry, the healthy parent should reassure the children that, for a time, they are going to have to pay attention to how loud they are and not try to annoy the suffering parent.
- The healthy parent should be proactive in measuring the effects by noticing if the children:
    1) are identifying with the trauma and showing signs of secondary trauma.
    2) are taking on a parental role and trying to rescue their wounded parent.
    3) are having problems at school such as depression, anxiety or having difficulties relating to friends.
- If any of these signs show up, it is time to get professional help from someone who knows how to deal with PTSD and its effects on the whole family.

What is ... the kind of action a parent might take which would make the situation worse?

(The healthy parent needs to know the best approaches to make.)

Answer:

- When a child is told not to discuss what he sees at home, he could develop anxiety because he has to always check himself, so he doesn't slip up and tell.

- When a child doesn't understand what is going on, then she is going to create her own ideas of what is happening, which may be a totally wrong impression.

- When a child is told or hears way too much information, he could develop symptoms of PTSD because of the terrible images he has in his head.

- When a child is given excuses for why the suffering parent is behaving strangely, she may learn to resolve issues later in life in a similar manner.

- When children know there is a cover-up, they could lose respect for their suffering parent. Also, they may not get a healthy perspective on the best way to act and react to an episode.

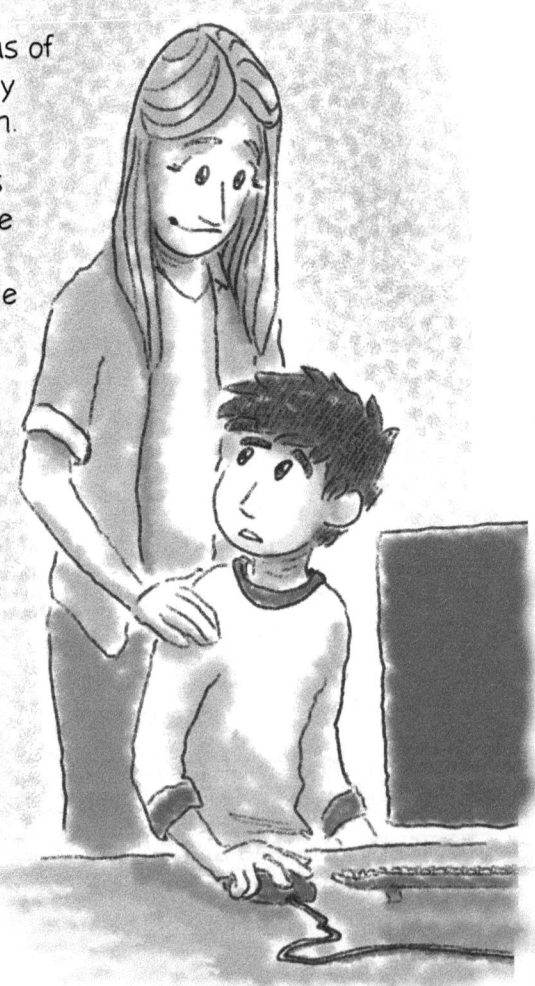

God's Words

When I Need Compassion

"Little children, let's not love with words or speech but with action and truth."

~ 1 John 3:18

"Love puts up with all things, trusts in all things, hopes for all things, endures all things."

~ 1 Corinthians 13:7

Discoveries

The Empowerment Check List Parents Can Use

Note: Young Readers, the following list is for your parents. Show it to them so they can use it to help keep the lines of communication open with you at all times.

_____ Answer kid questions with honesty and truth to the best of their ability to understand.
_____ Respond to kid questions with warmth, love, empathy and reassurance.
_____ Reassure children it's not their fault that their suffering parent is wounded.
_____ Reassure children the wounds will be healed soon.
_____ Use appropriate language for what is happening such as "hurt" instead of "injured."
_____ Explain that the war zone is real, not make-believe like violent movies, cartoons, video games or television programs.
_____ Make a frequent assessment of what is being comprehended by each child.
_____ Help the children understand that the PTSD symptoms are a common reaction to really bad experiences.
_____ Compare what is shared with life experiences the children have already had.
_____ Deal with all episodes that happen in the home in a positive way.
_____ Encourage children to freely express their concerns and feelings.
_____ Give lots of hugs no matter the age of the children..

POSITIVE ACTIVITIES

Note: After Sara's family shares about what happened to them, they will give everyone in the chapel a handout on prayer. They will briefly tell how specific prayers, using verses from the Bible, helped heal their family.

Sample Prayer for Parents to Pray for their Children

"Dear Lord, my child is having a hard time understanding why her/his wounded parent is acting so strangely right now. I pray _____ will know how much You love _____ and will rely on Your love daily (1 John 4:16). I pray for You to perform a miracle in _____'s heart and _____ will learn to come to You in confidence because You want to give mercy and grace to help in a great big time of need (Hebrews 4:15,16). Father, I pray _____ will have a forgiving heart, for You forgive us when we forgive those who sin against us.

Thank You for wanting to help my family. Amen"

Sample Prayer for the Wounded Parent

"Dear Lord, these are difficult times but I pray _____ will see that You want to carry all the burdens this PTSD brings with it (Psalm 68:19). I pray _____ will come to understand and believe You are faithful (Deuteronomy 7:9). I pray _____ will come to know that You love with an everlasting love (Jeremiah 31:3). I pray _____ will see that nothing is impossible with You and Your power to heal (Luke 1:37). I pray our family will know and understand Your authority in our lives.

Thank you for giving our family hope in this time of difficulty. Amen"

Sample Prayers for Christ-like Character

Compassion: "Dear Lord, I pray You will give all of us the compassion of Jesus and help us all to cope with the pain we see in our wounded parent. Help each of us to be able to reach out and bear with him." (Colossians 3:12)

Joy: "Dear Lord, I pray we will all experience the joy of the Lord, that Your Holy Spirit gives to those who welcome Your message even though there is suffering. Help us all to turn to You first and know where the joy comes from." (1 Thessalonians 1:6)

Obedient: "Dear Lord, I pray we will all become obedient in our walk with You. I pray we will all keep our eyes focused on You so no one becomes discouraged or depressed. Help all of us show respect and love for each member of the family, just as Jesus showed respect and love to You." (Hebrews 5:8)

Peace-loving: "Dear Lord, I pray each member of our family tries very hard to do what leads to peace in all situations. I pray we act positively towards each other instead of being critical. I pray we go out of our way to be encouraging instead of causing problems. Help us as we show a great deal of patience while we wait for Your complete healing." (Romans 14:19)

Self-Control: "Dear Lord, I pray my family wants to remain alert and show self-control daily. I pray we would live by the Spirit by expressing much love, joy, peace, patience, kindness, goodness, faithfulness, gentleness and self-control because we belong to Christ. Help my family walk in the Spirit." (Galatians 5:22,23)

Servant's Heart: "Dear Lord, I pray you will give each member in my family a servant's heart. I pray we would desire to serve each other as if we were serving You. Help us to show love and honor towards each other as good examples of how You love us." (Ephesians 6:7)

Sara's Prayer

"Dear God, thank You for the strength You give every day to help us, guide us, encourage us and keep our paths straight. Help us walk in such a way that others may know who You are and why we believe in You. Thank You for all You have done to get our family on the right track while we experienced PTSD. Help us speak the truth in love whenever we are asked how we did it. You are the best! Amen"

  The Important Life Value is:

Compassion
(definition: a feeling of deep sympathy and sorrow for another person suffering from an affliction)

We desire to reach out to anyone who asks how God helped us get through the PTSD problem. We want to be used by Him as we continue to grow in knowledge and understanding of the Christian faith.

signed, Sara, Mom, Dad and Jacob

How Will It End?

Chapter 13
Story by Jenna

The chapel service was packed with lots of people. I don't think there was an open seat left in the room. The word went out throughout the whole base that a wounded warrior and his family were going to be the star speakers for the day. My mom, dad, little brother and I were on the front row, sitting next to Sara's and Jacob's family. We were there to cheer them on. The eager reporter and his camera crew were all set up waiting for the service to begin.

After some great worship music with live musicians, Chaplain Johnson finally stood up to speak. He gave a short introduction about what would happen next. "Folks, the best part about my job is when I witness the work of God in a person's life. Such a change has happened in the life of one of our wounded warriors, who was diagnosed with Post-Traumatic Stress Disorder a number of months ago. He and his family are here to share their story of healing. Not only was he changed in a dramatic way, his family is here to tell their part of the story too. Let's welcome them to the stage, please."

After a rousing round of applause, Sara's family were all seated on their stools, each holding a microphone, and the story-sharing began.

"Are you sure you know who your enemy is?" Sara's dad started with a question. "When I came back from my latest deployment, I thought I had left the enemy back in the desert when I walked away from the fighting and headed home." He continued to tell everyone about his discoveries of how Satan had been working to keep him from turning to God in his time of need. In great detail he told about his six-month journey to find the best enemy-fighting force available anywhere. He said if someone had not told him about the healing power of Jesus, he and his family would not be sitting here today. He gave credit to Chaplain Johnson and to my dad for coming alongside him at his greatest need. What a good feeling it was to know our family helped Sara's family. Sara's eyes met mine and we smiled shyly at each other.

Sara told of the traumatic episode she had when she witnessed the gun aimed at her mom.

Next, she told about her experience with the negative note she had received from some girls at school. "I came to realize that whoever sent it knew nothing about what had really happened. At first I was very sad, but it gave me an opportunity to speak to our whole school on the subject of PTSD from a kid's point of view," Sara said.

She then pointed to me sitting in the front row and said, "My best friend, Jenna, and I have done research on how families can be affected by PTSD. Some parents, who have been deployed, may not even know they have some of the symptoms. When we spoke at our school recently, there were some students who stopped us in the hall and told us their dad or mom seemed to be acting just as we described.

"It is not easy, but when someone needs help, they should talk to Chaplain Johnson about what can be done."

After Sara's mom spoke about the importance of having a community of friends around in a time of need, Jacob ended the sharing time by reading his paper called, "My Hero." The story he read was about why his dad was a hero and why he wanted to go into the military someday, just like his dad. Everyone cheered loudly and clapped when he was done.

The service came to an end and many people came up to congratulate Sara's family. They thanked them for talking about their experiences. Some ladies were crying and lots of hugs were happening. Finally, when we were all walking out to the cars in the parking lot, two girls from our school came walking towards Sara and me.

"Sara, can we talk to you, please?" one of them said.

"Sure," she said, as they came closer.

"We are the ones who sent you that nasty note in school and we want to apologize. We're really sorry we hurt you like that," one of them said.

Just then, Sara's mom and my mom walked up and heard what the girls were saying.

"I didn't understand what had happened to your dad, until you spoke to the whole school about ... What do you call that again?" one of the girls asked.

"Post-Traumatic Stress Disorder," I said quickly.

Sara's mom asked the girls "Were you and your families in the service just now?"

"Yes, we really liked what you had to say, especially telling about how your whole family had turned to God during this time. My mom and dad have just started coming to chapel, and I am so glad we heard your stories today," one of the girls said with a smile.

"So Sara, what do you want to say to these nice girls after their apology?" asked Mom.

"I forgive you and accept your apology. What are your names? We didn't have many classes together last year but maybe we will when school begins again," Sara exclaimed with a big smile.

When the girls' parents caught up to us, my dad found out who they were and what units in the military they were serving with. He said to them, "We are all on our way to a backyard BBQ. Would you like to join us?"

That summer changed all of our lives. Sara and I became friends with the two girls from school who wrote the nasty note. We discovered we had a lot in common and had the best time together. Jacob made friends with one of the girl's brothers who also likes to skateboard. All the moms and dads became great friends too. Most weekends, we traded off whose home we went to for a BBQ.

The young reporter and his wife also became a part of the BBQ crowd. When he showed the segment on TV about Sara's family telling their story, he told us that the positive response was enormous. His boss asked him to do a whole hour on the subject of PTSD and how it affects the entire family.

Through this experience, I have begun to learn how important it is to have a life turned to God. I really like it and can't wait to learn more every day. Best of all, Sara, Jacob and I have already made plans to talk to more students about PTSD. The more young people who know about it, the better it is. And, of course, we know God promises to help us with our plans wherever and whatever they are. Of that, we are sure!!

What is...

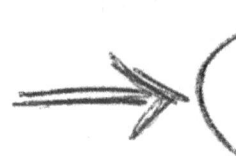 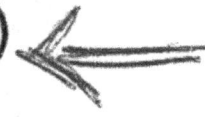

different in Sara's family since the gun incident?

(the changes as a result of the PTSD and the healing)

Answer: The Work of God

Where there once was...	There is now...	Because of...	Verses
fear	trust in God	God's strength	Psalm 28:7
sadness	confidence in God's plan	God's saving presence	Romans 15:13
isolation	fellowship with God	God's protection	Psalm 23:4
lack of forgiveness	kindness & compassion	God's forgiveness	Ephesians 4:32
lack of direction	willingness to wait on God	God's inspiration	2 Timothy 3:16
misunderstanding	taking time to think	God's instructions	2 Timothy 2:7
no relationship with God	relationship with God	God's love	John 3:16
lack of sensitivity	understanding of sin	God's encouragement	Hebrews 3:13
weakness	endurance to the end	God's power	Philippians 4:13
lack of strength	strong support	God's shield	Psalm 18:35
discouragement	heart filled with courage	God's greatness	Psalm 31:24
lack of compassion	love and trust	God's hope	1 Corinthians 13:7
hopelessness	joy & peace in faith	God's gift of Holy Spirit	Romans 15:13

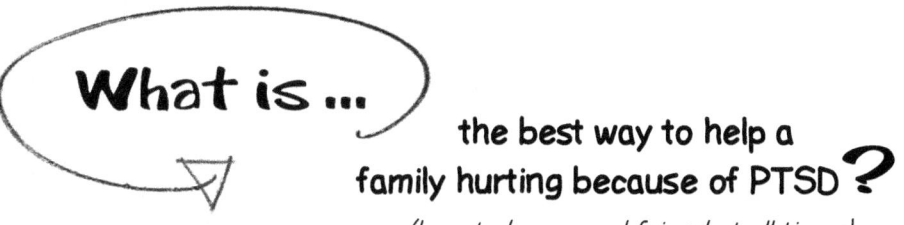

What is ... the best way to help a family hurting because of PTSD?

(how to be a good friend at all times)

Answer:

- Be educated on the subject, and be ready to educate others.
- Treat those suffering as wounded and not crazy.
- Let it be known that God is the Greatest Healer.
- Think positive about every situation, but be patient when others feel hopeless.
- Be a good listener, but keep what you know private.
- Be sensitive yet understanding.
- Pray consistently and regularly.
- Be truthful and not judgmental.

God's Words

When I Need Hope

"Be happy in your hope, stand your ground when you're in trouble, and devote yourselves to prayer."

~ Romans 12:12

"I will give thanks to You, God, forever, because You have acted. In the presence of Your faithful people, I will hope in Your name because it's so good."

~ Psalm 52:9

Discoveries

The Work of the Holy Spirit

Note: When you invite Jesus to have a relationship with you, He sends the Holy Spirit to be with you. The Holy Spirit guides you when making decisions, encourages you when you are down and helps you to be obedient. You are not a robot because your decisions are **your** decisions. The Holy Spirit guides you to make the best kind of decisions; however, He is not going to force you. It is God's plan for you to allow the Holy Spirit to influence you in a positive way. By doing so, your life will be made richer and fuller.

Without Christ, God, or Holy Spirit	With Christ, God, or Holy Spirit	With Christ But Going My Own Way
I am in control of my own life	Christ is guiding my life	I control my life instead of Christ
Christ is outside of my life	Walk closely to God and His ways	Ignore God's ways
Frustration in my life	Seek love, joy, peace, patience	Show anger, chaos, impatience
Never think about God in my life	Seek to be kind, good and faithful	Show lack of self-control

How do I get Christ in?

Note: Look up each verse and write one way you can get "I" out and Christ in.

Steps	Verse
Must be truly willing to obey God's ways	Matthew 5:6
Must ask God to reveal any sins and confess them	1 John 1:9
Must be committed to God's will in my life	Romans 6:16-18
Must be active in asking God for help in obeying	Luke 11:9-13
Must believe & have a heart of thankfulness	Mark 11:24

POSITIVE ACTIVITIES

Note: When we have Christ in our lives, the work we do because of Him is as if He is doing the work. Sara, Jacob and Jenna want to use their experiences to help others. Christ is a good example of a willing heart who wants to help. Just look at what He did on the cross. Now, let's look at some things the three kids can do because He is in their lives.

- Ask the youth leader of their church to put together projects kids can do for those who are deployed. For example: write letters, collect items for care packages, make cookies to sell to raise funds for postage.

- Ask parents to see if neighborhood families suffering from PTSD/Combat Trauma need their lawns mowed, weeds pulled, etc.

- Ask a favorite teacher to help them reach out to new military students.

- As a family, be a part of local community projects that aid and assist military families in need.

- Ask your parents to talk to youth leaders from many churches in your neighborhood to suggest all of them give free car washes for military families, distribute holiday food baskets, etc.

Jenna's Prayer

"Dear God, help us be ones who love You more every day. Thank You for the way You work in our lives. Thank You, too, for all of Your plans, and that we can be a part of them. We ask for Your wisdom as we trust You with our very lives. We ask for Your guidance in our quest to help others whose parents have PTSD symptoms. We love You! Amen"

 The Important Life Value is:

Hope
(definition: the feeling that what is wanted can be had)

I want to know God more because I see that, when I do, my life can have a purpose. I desire to make my life count for God, and to be there to give hope to other kids my age.

signed, Jenna

Appendix

Appendix for Parents

- **Chapter One**
  "Failure to Scream" by Robert Hicks [Thomas Nelson, 1993]
  "When God Doesn't Make Sense" by Dr. James C. Dobson [Living Books, 2001]

- **Chapter Two**
  "In Harm's Way: Help for the Wives of Military Men, Police, EMT's & Firefighters" by Aphrodite Matsakis, Ph.D. [New Harbinger Publications, 2005]
  "Veterans and Families' Guide to Recovering from PTSD" by Stephanie Laite Lanham [Purple Heart Service Foundation, 2007, www.purpleheartfoundation.org or email: phsf@purpleheartfoundation.org]

- **Chapter Three**
  "Turn My Mourning Into Dancing: Finding Hope in Hard Times" by Henri Nouwen [Word Publishing/Thomas Nelson, 2001]
  "When War Comes Home: Christ-centered Healing for Wives of Combat Veterans" by Chris and Rahnella Adsit and Marshele Carter Waddell [Military Ministry Press, 2008]

- **Chapter Four**
  "The New Freedom of Forgiveness" by David Augsburger [Moody Press, 2001]
  "When You Can't Say 'I Forgive You'" by Grace Ketterman & David Hazard [NavPress, 2000]

- **Chapter Five**
  "The Domestic Violence Sourcebook" by Dawn Bradley Berry, J.D. [Lowell House, 2000]
  "When Love Hurts" by Jill Cory & Karen McAndless-Davis [WomenKind Press, 2003]

- **Chapter Six**
  "Connecting With God" by Chris Adsit [Disciplemakers International, 2001]
  "Loving Your Military Man" by Beatrice Fishback [Family Life Publishing, 2007]

- **Chapter Seven**
    "31 Days of Praise" by Ruth Myers [Multnomah Books, 1994]
    "Who Calls Me Beautiful? Finding Our True Image in the Mirror of God" by Regina Franklin [Discovery House Publishers, 2004]

- **Chapter Eight**
    "Hope for the Home Front" by Marshele Carter Waddell [One Hope Ministry, 2003]
    "Two Hearts Praying as One" by Dennis & Barbara Rainey [Multnomah Publishers, 2002]

- **Chapter Nine**
    "Christlife: Identifying Your True and Deepest Identity" by Ruth Myers [Multnomah, 2005]
    "Roll Away Your Stone" by Dutch Sheets [Bethany, 2007]

- **Chapter Ten**
    "The Adversary: The Christian Versus Demon Activity" by Mark I. Bubeck [Moody Press, 1975]
    "A Woman's Guide to Spiritual Warfare" by Quin Sherrer and Ruthanne Garlock [Servant Publications, 1991]

- **Chapter Eleven**
    "Intercessory Prayer" by Dutch Sheets [Regal Books, 1996]
    "Prayers That Avail Much" by Germaine Copeland [Harrison House, 1997]

- **Chapter Twelve**
    "How to Pray for Your Children" by Quin Sherrer [Regal Books, 1998]
    "The Seduction of Our Children" by Neil T. Anderson and Steve Russo [Harvest House Publishers, 1991]

- **Chapter Thirteen**
    "Courage After Fire" by Keith Armstrong, L.C.S.W., Suzanne Best, PhD., Paula Domenici, PhD. [Ulysses Press, 2006]
    "Defending the Military Marriage" by Lt. Col. Jim and Beatrice Fishback [Family Life Publishing, 2004]
    "Defending the Military Family" by Lt. Col. Jim and Beatrice Fishback [Family Life Publishing, 2005]

Appendix for Young Readers

"Brats: Our Journey Home" by Bridget Musil and narrated by Kris Kristofferson [Brats Without Borders, 2005] 90-minute documentary (DVD) presents "What it is like growing up as a military brat."

"My Book About the War and Terrorism: A guided activity workbook for children, families and teachers to encourage healthy expression, learning and coping" by Gilbert Kliman, M.D., Harriet Wolfe, M.D.; Edward Oklan, M.D.; M.P.H. [The Children's Psychological Health Center, Inc., 2003] www.cphc-sf.org

"Quest: A Kid's Journey Through Deployment" by Beatrice Fishback and Elizabeth Tyrrell [Military Ministry Press, 2013]

"Why Is Daddy Like He Is?" By Patience Mason [Patience Press, 1992]

www.ingramcontent.com/pod-product-compliance
Lightning Source LLC
Chambersburg PA
CBHW070503100426
42743CB00010B/1735